Black Powder, Pig Lead and Steel Silhouettes

Brian Chilson (left) presenting the High Senior plaque to the author on June 25, 2000, at the Ridgway Rifle Club silhouette range. For that match, Paul used an O.T.A. Hepburn built by Ron Snover. The load was an original design 540-grain Postell bullet cast 0.455 inch diameter in a Steve Brooks mould backed by 67 grains of GOEX FFg powder, 0.060 inch thick Walters vegetable fiber wad and fired by a Winchester WLRM primer in a Federal premium cartridge case.

Black Powder, Pig Lead and Steel Silhouettes

by

Paul A. Matthews

Wolfe Publishing Company

2625 Stearman Road, Suite A
Prescott, Arizona 86301

Printed in the United States of America

06 05 04 03   5 4 3 2 1

Published November 2002

ISBN: 1-879356-60-0

This little book is dedicated to
black powder cartridge rifle shooters everywhere.
To a person, you are the greatest people I have
ever met, people with old-time, traditional values
of honesty, integrity and loyalty. May you forever
grace and enjoy this great nation.

Warning

This book contains practices and procedures used in the reloading and shooting of black-powder cartridges. As far as can be determined, these practices and procedures were carried out in a safe manner and gave no indication of potential problems relative to safety. However, since neither I nor the publisher of this book have any control over the manner or methods by which you might follow some of these practices and procedures, nor do we have any control over the quality or condition of your equipment, rifles, ammunition or components, we hereby disclaim all possible liability for damage to equipment or injury to any person as a result of reader usage of information or advice within this book. If you choose to use any or all of the information or advice contained in this book, do so with caution and with the knowledge you are strictly on your own and you assume all responsibility for your actions.

Paul A. Matthews

March 18, 2002

Contents

Preface

I have been shooting a rifle ever since I was five years old and have owned at least one rifle every day of my life since March 17, 1935, when my older brother Wilfrid received a new Springfield Model 86 .22 rimfire rifle for his birthday, and his little $3 Sears Roebuck rifle chambered for the .22 short cartridge was passed on to me. The little rifle was a piece of junk, but I cherished it until I received my own Springfield Model 86A a few years later.

I did not begin to take rifles seriously until just after World War II, and although I played with black powder and cast bullets in those early years, I really did not take that seriously until June 1992 when, at the age of 66, I fired my first black powder cartridge rifle silhouette match at Ridgway, Pennsylvania. Out of 40 targets, I hit three! What a humbling experience!

It is my personal opinion that of all the various shooting disciplines in existence in this year of 2002 A.D. that of the black powder cartridge rifle silhouettes is the most demanding. I am certain those who participate in the black-powder rifle long-range shooting – 800, 900 and 1,000 yards – will make the same claim for their sport, and I will not argue too heavily against them as long as they use a straight charge of black powder with no smokeless duplexing and plain base lead alloy bullets with no gas checks affixed to the base of the bullet.

I make this claim for the BPCR silhouette shooter because of the traditionalist requirements of the sport – the exposed hammer, a single-shot rifle originally manufactured in the United States chambered for a black-powder cartridge, iron sights typical of those used in the late 1800s and, of course, cartridges loaded with a charge of straight black powder and a lead alloy bullet.

On the surface it all looks very simple. But I challenge any shooter who has not tried it to purchase his own black-powder rifle, select the bullet style he believes will give the best performance and then buy the mould, cast the bullets, load the ammunition with black powder and go to the range and shoot. When one starts to cast his own bullets and load them in front of black powder with the objective of making them shoot into minute and a half or less at 547 yards, then he or she begins to scratch the surface of what this is all about!

Not only are some of these black powder cartridge rifles fussy about the style of bullet, they are also fussy about the diameter of the driving bands and the diameter of the nose in front of the driving bands. Where almost any good cast bullet can be made to deliver good performance in the deer woods or on the 100-yard target out back of the barn, it is a whole different ball game when you stretch the distance to 547 yards, throw in an 11- to 13-foot trajectory, add a few fitful gusts of wind and change the light conditions from shot to shot.

Shooting under such conditions at the silhouettes, whether it be at the pigs at 328 yards, the turkeys at 421 yards or the rams at 547 yards, soon lets you know just how much you don't know about riflery. It is one thing to borrow someone else's rifle and ammunition and shoot a good score; it is something else to start from scratch with your own rifle and ammunition and try to shoot a good score. On more than one occasion, I have known of a shooter coming to his first BPCR silhouette match using the rifle and ammunition of his partner who was an experienced silhouette shooter. Usually the first time shooter would shoot a good score. But when he showed up at the next match with his own rifle and his own loads, his score was significantly lower.

One other factor that makes BPCR silhouette shooting so unique is the fact the targets are not symmetrical nor do you shoot at the same target twice for score. Whereas the long-range BPCR shooter has a target with a round bullseye that makes a perfect center for an aperature front sight, and he shoots at the same target time after time for score, the BPCR silhouette shooter fires his sighter shots at one target and then fires each successive shot for score at a different target. While this might not seem too big a deal, the angle of reflection off each target is different. With iron sights this gives the shooter a subtle difference in perspective on each target, a difference that can be multiplied several times under changing light conditions.

To further complicate the angle of reflection off each target, not all targets – especially the chickens and turkeys – are placed on their respective stands at the same angle relative to the shooter. This changes the angle of reflection even more, and many a shooter has scratched his head wondering what went wrong with a shot when the sight picture and trigger squeeze were so perfect.

As for targets not being symmetrical, I believe it was Francis Sell who once wrote that an aperature front sight was the worst of all to be used on a hunting rifle because targets were not symmetrical. At the time I doubted Sell's wisdom and put a beautiful rugged gold-faced aperature front sight on my Ruger No. 3 .45-70 in place of the ⅛-inch post I normally used. One offhand session at the range using a full-size deer target at 100 yards proved Sell to be correct.

Only by 100 percent concentration on sight picture and trigger squeeze can the BPCR silhouette shooter keep his shots on an irregular shaped target whose maximum area might be a horizontal oblong as on the pigs and rams, or a slightly tilted football shape as on the turkeys, or as on that squat chicken shape that has to be taken offhand at 218 yards. With these targets there is no such thing as an intermediate score point such as a 3 or a 4. On the contrary, in the silhouette game each shot is either a one or a zero – you either knock the target from its stand or you score a miss even when you manage to hit the target, but for some reason known only to the gods, the target remains standing.

This type of scoring – either knock down or miss – makes the use of the less powerful black-powder cartridges a chancy thing, a demand for even greater skill on the part of the shooter.

For all the years I have shot and hunted with a rifle, I was never interested in competitive shooting until that day in June 1992 when I discovered that black powder cartridge rifle silhouette competition demanded a whole lot more than just plain good shooting. Now, as I approach my 75th birthday, I try to put on paper what I have learned about the sport in hopes that others will be able to use it and that I will be able to continue shooting long enough to learn even more.

1

Over the Cross-Sticks

Many of us learn by accident. Call it experience if you will, but much of it is experience brought about by pure accident. Like what happened to me on June 28, 1998, during the Pennsylvania State Championship BPCR silhouette match held at Ridgway, Pennsylvania.

A lot of shooters, myself among them at that time, choose not to get involved in making a long run on any particular target during a match. It is simply too tiring to attempt a long run on the turkeys or rams during the match due to the amount of competitive pressure and concentration required to hit all of a given target for score and then to keep on going until you miss, in hopes of setting a new national record for the number of animals knocked over. With the pigs it is somewhat different in that long runs on pigs are usually done after the match due to the potential for a high number of hits.

With me, the reluctance to get into a long run was even greater than normal. I was 72 at the time, and just the act of shooting a 60-round match totally exhausted me. So after knocking down all 15 pigs to finish the match with a score of 38, I declined nephew Eric's suggestion that I make an attempt at a long run.

"But Uncle Paul," he said, "you've only got to hit 10 more pigs to tie the national record!" Thus it was that after the match I took my equipment back to the line and prepared for the long run.

I have always been fussy about getting my cross-sticks adjusted to a height that makes it comfortable for me to shoot. But on this day, for some unknown reason, perhaps fatigue, when I was given the command READY, I realized my cross-sticks were much lower than usual. I could not support the rifle against my right shoulder with my left elbow on the shooting mat and my left hand on my right shoulder supporting the toe of the stock.

Not wanting to spend precious time resetting my cross-sticks, I made a fist of my left hand and placed it on the shooting mat with the toe of the stock resting in the small curl formed by my forefinger and thumb. Then I cheeked the stock and put on just enough downward pressure to raise the muzzle and bring my pig into the center of the front aperture sight. The rifle hung there as though set in concrete, and I tipped each pig on the bank with an ease I had never known before.

The targets were reset and I started again, but this time my number four pig fell over due to wind or unbalance before I got to him. So after taking the rest of the pigs on that bank, the range master asked if I would shoot at the number one pig on the adjacent bank in place of the number four pig that had fallen down. This I agreed to even though it extended the distance by a few feet. As expected, I hit the pig low in the belly and, in the process, tied the national senior record.

While the targets were being reset, that low shot nagged at me, and when I was called to the line again, I raised my sight half a point and fired at the number one pig on the new bank. It was my 26th shot, and it went over the back by half an inch. I had tied the senior record for a long run on the pigs, but I had failed to set a new record.

I was a far better shooter coming out of that long run attempt than I was going in. Most importantly, I learned to get my body as flat to the mat as possible while still supporting the toe of the stock with my hand. When you are shooting, regardless of position, the body is nothing more nor less than a shooting platform, and a flat rock in the cow pasture is a lot more stable than a three-legged milk stool in the barn. The higher you prop yourself up on your elbows to accommodate the cross-sticks, the less stable you are.

As for the cross-sticks themselves, from that day to this the height of my cross-sticks from ground level to pivot bolt is recorded on my sight setting card for every range I shoot on and for each bank of targets except chickens. I carry a steel measuring tape in my equipment box to check the height of my cross-sticks when I set them. This saves me all kinds of time in getting the cross-sticks set at the proper height for comfortable shooting and assures that the line of recoil is always the same no matter where I shoot nor what target I shoot at.

Now I realize that most shooters pay little attention to the exact height of cross-sticks. They go to the line, thrust their cross-sticks into the ground and go to the task of shooting. Once in awhile a shooter will reposition his sticks, but almost never do I see another shooter actually measure the height of his cross-sticks as I do.

If there is any one reason I am so fussy about the height of my cross-sticks, it is the fact that in this game of BPCR silhouette competition I have learned that uniformity begets uniformity. That philosophy applies to the height of your cross-sticks just as it applies to powder charge, bullet weight or powder compression. It applies to everything you do relative to BPCR silhouette competition.

One other thing I learned by accident on that June 28, 1998, was to pay more attention to the trajectory of my bullets relative to the distance I was shooting. As mentioned earlier, I was not at all surprised when my shot at number one pig on the adjacent bank hit low in the belly. After all, the pig in the adjacent bank was a few feet (yards?) farther away. But just how much difference does a few feet make?

While one cannot answer this question with an exact figure, one can say that for every 25 yards of additional range between 300 and 600 yards, you can elevate your rear sight about three points or three minutes, whichever term you prefer to use. That works out to one minute of added elevation for every 25 *feet* of additional distance. Whatever the case, one thing is certain: I should *not* have raised my sight that extra half minute when I went back to number one pig on my own bank! That cost me!

With these new lessons learned, I was at the Ridgway rifle range again on July 25 and 26 of that same year for the Eastern Regional Championship silhouette match. And again, on the 26th, I scored on all 15 pigs and went for a long run. This time I knocked over 59 pigs before missing number 60, and by the time I was finished shooting, the sun was approaching the horizon and the shadows behind the pigs made them look almost twice their actual length.

Cross-sticks are a critical part of your equipment. They are the traditional means of supporting your rifle barrel while shooting prone or sitting. And once I corresponded with a gentleman of South Africa who regularly used a set of cross-sticks to shoot from the standing position while hunting. In the tall grass, he said they were a big asset. His standing cross-sticks were made of two half-round pieces with a pivot screw or rivet about shirt pocket high. When not in use for supporting the rifle, a rubber cap as used on a crutch kept the cross-sticks together at the bottom so they could be used as a walking stick.

As critical as cross-sticks are, a lot of shooters pay little attention to the rigidity of them once they are stuck into the ground. While it is not always possible, due to the type of soil at the range, to set the sticks deeply enough to eliminate movement as the rifle is set into place, one should take the time to get his cross-sticks set as solidly as possible. It will help you get a better score just as it helped the old buffalo hunters fire fewer cartridges for each animal taken.

2

Observations of the Bullet

One of the best bullets I ever used was a copy of the original Lyman Postell bullet designated as No. 457132 and weighing 535 grains. From what I read at one time, this bullet was a grooved version of the old Sharps 550-grain paper patched bullet. It was developed especially for long-range shooting and was produced by Lyman in its original form for many years before being slightly modified in design in 1974 according to a drawing I have.

My first acquaintance with the Postell bullet came in 1950 when I ordered a mould from Lyman with the cavity cut short by one driving band and one grease groove. My intent at that time was to use the bullet in an 1886 lever-action Winchester, and this I did though I had to seat the bullet deeply in the cartridge case in order for it to function through the magazine. I also fired a few rounds with this bullet through a Sharps-Borchardt with superb accuracy.

In later years when I first got into black powder cartridge rifle silhouettes, I used this 475-grain version of the Postell for my first 14 BPCR silhouette matches and my one and only 1,000-yard BPCR match held at

Bodines, Pennsylvania, in July 1993. These matches were all fired using a Navy Arms rolling block .45-70 on which the barrel had been set back and rechambered by John Korzinek, riflesmith of Canton, Pennsylvania.

At that time I was using RS Pyrodex as a propellant and have to say it and the Postell bullet gave excellent performance, better than the capabilities of the man behind the buttstock! However, beginning with match No. 26 through match No. 40, I started sifting my RS Pyrodex through a tea strainer to get all the "fines" out of it.

Getting back to bullets, late in the 1994 season, having decided the 475-grain version of the Postell was too vulnerable to wind, I had Tom Ballard cut me a new mould to cast a 550-grain Postell bullet. This was a fine mould, and I used this bullet almost exclusively right up through August 1999 when I switched to the same bullet cast from a Steve Brooks bullet mould.

The reason I changed from the Tom Ballard mould to the Steve Brooks mould was a matter of cast bullet diameter. During the early years of my BPCR shooting, I pretty much followed the old adage that one used a cast bullet that was about one thousandth (0.001) inch larger than the groove diameter of one's barrel. Thus all my bullets went through a .459-inch sizing die in my SAECO lubri-sizer. This just nicely cleaned up the driving bands of my original 475-grain Postell bullet.

For some unknown reason, perhaps curiosity, during the 1994 season I discovered that sizing my bullets down to .458 inch improved their accuracy, and that sizing them down to .4575 inch provided an additional improvement. Why this was to be was beyond my knowledge at the time. But because it was a fact borne out in actual practice, I ordered a new Postell bullet mould from Tom Ballard that would cast .4575 inch over the driving bands. At the same time, I ordered a nose-pour version of the Lyman 457125 bullet from Dave Farmer of Colorado Shooter's Supply. This, too, was to cast .4575 inch over the driving bands.

I received the Tom Ballard mould first, just about the same time I received my new rolling block .45-70 from Ron Snover of IXL Enterprises. Right from the beginning with my 29th silhouette match, it seemed the bullet from that specific mould was meant for the new rifle. It was a winning combination, though I had no idea why an undersize bullet should give superlative accuracy.

In the fall of 1998, I switched from Remington cartridge cases to Federal premium grade nickel-plated cases. This in itself seemed insignificant at the time, though in the course of taking several measurements of the new cases, it was readily apparent the Federal cases had a thicker wall than the Remingtons. Whereas the wall thickness of a Remington case was ten thousandths (0.010) inch at the mouth of the case, that of the Federal's was eleven thousandths (0.011) inch. *On a fireformed case this meant the Federal cases were two thousandths (0.002) inch smaller on the inside diameter than were the Remington cases!* It also meant my Tom Ballard Postell bullet that cast .4575 inch diameter was a snug fit in a fireformed Federal case, and just maybe there was not sufficient clearance between the bullet and cartridge case at the instant of firing.

It did not take too long to put some of those Tom Ballard Postell bullets through a .455-inch lubri-sizing die and learn that when fired from a Federal cartridge case, a .455-inch bullet shot better than a .4575-inch bullet! That was when I ordered a new bullet mould from Steve Brooks to cast a Postell bullet exactly like the Tom Ballard Postell except that it was to measure .455 inch diameter over the driving bands when cast.

By this time I am certain it is obvious I prefer to shoot my bullets as nearly to their "as cast" diameter as possible. I do this because when you size a bullet, you distort it to some degree. Distortion, regardless of how little, is detrimental to accuracy. Thus, when lubricating these bullets, they are put through a size-to-size die, and sometimes through a slightly oversized die. In either case, there is very little or no resizing done to my bullets prior to loading, and I believe this helps in obtaining their full potential in the accuracy department.

Although I had determined the optimum diameter of my Postell bullets by trial and error, such an approach is costly and time-consuming. If I were starting all over again with a new rifle, the first thing on the agenda would be to forget those old adages that "cast bullets should be one thousandth (0.001) larger than the groove diameter of the barrel" or that "cast bullets should be the same diameter as the throat of the barrel" or that "undersize cast bullets will lead your barrel," etc.

These old wives tales might hold true for shooting smallbore cast bullets backed by smokeless powder in high-powered rifles. But we are dealing with black-powder cartridges in black powder cartridge rifles, and almost every shooter with a head full of gray hair has at one time or another loaded a cartridge for an original black-powder rifle and discovered that when he seated a groove-diameter bullet in the cartridge case, the cartridge would not chamber! In short, there were many, many original black powder cartridge rifles purposely chambered for undersized bullets! And they gave superb accuracy!

Knowing all this, the second thing on the agenda when determining proper bullet diameter for a new rifle is to take a fireformed cartridge case from that rifle and, after carefully chamfering the mouth of the case to remove any leftover crimp or burr, carefully measure the inside diameter of the mouth of the case. Then size your bullets two to three thousandths (0.002 to 0.003) inch smaller than the inside diameter of the mouth of the cartridge case. This will allow the cartridge case to completely release the bullet at the instant of firing.

Most of us are well aware of the fact that cast bullets fired from a black powder cartridge rifle start to "bump up" or "upset" at the instant of powder ignition and, according to tests by Dr. Franklin W. Mann using a shortened .32-40 cartridge case, the upsettage occurs fully and completely within the chamber. While I do not question Dr. Mann's conclusion for this specific test, I do believe the rate of upsettage can and will vary with bullet hardness, powder granulation, resiliency of the wad used and probably even the make of powder used. In fact, in other tests by Dr. Mann, he proved bullet upsettage continued for about the first 10 inches of barrel.

What all this adds up to is that with a black powder cartridge rifle and cast bullets, just as with a high-powered rifle and metal jacketed bullets, the dimensions of the chamber, cartridge case and bullet must be such that upon the instant of firing the walls of the cartridge case must be able to expand sufficiently enough to completely release the bullet. If this does not happen, you will get erratic pressures and velocity with subsequent loss in accuracy.

Now, getting back to the Postell bullet, it was originally designed for long-range target work and, according to the *Ideal Handbook No. 13*, was first made by the Ideal Manufacturing Company for George R. Russell of Boston and was first used at Seagirt by the Boston military companies.

The design of the present-day Postell bullet is slightly changed from the original. Bullets from my old 1950 mould had a nose diameter of .443 inch just ahead of the front driving band, while another original design Postell bullet had a diameter of .441 inch at this location. On bullets of the original design, the ogive started immediately ahead of the front driving band and made one long, sweeping radius that terminated in a fine streamlined roundnose.

In 1974, according to a drawing dated March 29 of that year, the nose shape was changed by the then Leisure Group, Inc. to provide a straight parallel-sided section two-tenths (0.2) inch long immediately ahead of the front driving band. The diameter of this section was maintained at .441 inch. This drawing is stamped "Obsolete" dated July 30, 1991.

A few years later when Lyman Products, Inc. reinstated the Postell bullet under its original number 457132, the diameter of the parallel-sided section was increased to .450 inch to make it a true bore-riding nose. Though I much prefer the original design for shooting through a powder-fouled barrel, I have seen the new designed bullet give superb accuracy in a number of rifles.

Although I believe the original design Postell bullet is one of the best – if not the best – long-range bullet ever designed for the .45-caliber rifle, I also believe that its long streamline design *might* make it more vulnerable to wind at the longer ranges than a shorter, blunter bullet of the same or nearly same weight. I believe this because of the simple fact the longer a bullet is for a given weight and diameter, the faster you have to spin that bullet in order to stabilize it. And at the longer ranges where the bullet's linear velocity has slowed, its rotational velocity has also slowed, perhaps not enough to destabilize it, but enough to make it more vulnerable to wind.

The .45-70 cartridge case, in my opinion, does not have sufficient powder capacity to drive 535- to 550-grain Postell bullets at high enough muzzle velocity to assure optimum stability at the longer ranges. And when the stability of a bullet begins to deteriorate, then that bullet becomes more vulnerable to wind.

Early on in the BPCR silhouette game, I had purchased a new mould for the Lyman 457125 bullet. This bullet weighed 525 grains and was 1.309 inches long, ⅛ inch shorter than my Postell. However, the nose diameter followed the modern trend of smallbore high-powered rifle cast bullets in that it had a bore-riding diameter of .450 inch and did not shoot well in my rifle. In a phone conversation with Bill Casteel at that time, I learned he had a similar mould but did not like it because the diameter of the nose was too small – .448 inch. We traded moulds and for the next 14 BPCR silhouette matches, I used the Lyman 457125 bullet from Bill Casteel's mould.

This bullet showed a lot of promise, but because its cast diameter was .459 to .460 inch over the driving bands, and I was sizing it down to .4575 inch, I ordered a nose-pour mould for this bullet from Dave Farmer of Colorado Shooter's Supply. The new bullet was to cast

.4575 inch over the driving bands and .447 inch in front of the front driving band. While this mould was in the process of being made, I started using my new Tom Ballard Postell bullet, and immediately my scores improved. I started using the Tom Ballard Postell at Wilton, New York, on March 12, 1995, and with the exception of four matches continued to use it through December 12, 1999.

As soon as I received the nose-pour 457125 bullet mould from Dave Farmer, I cast a batch of bullets with it for testing. Dave makes excellent bullet moulds, and the bullets from this mould cast exactly to the dimensions I had specified. But for some reason unknown to me at that time, the bullet did not perform as expected, and the mould was oiled and put away. After all, I had a superb bullet in the Ballard Postell, and whether or not the roundnose 457125 bullet performed well seemed of little consequence.

After making a successful long run on the pigs – 59 pigs – on July 26, 1998, and becoming a co-holder of the senior long run record on the rams that same day – 10 rams – I made up my mind I would work toward setting a new senior and open long run record on the rams. But try as I did for the rest of the 1998 season and all of the 1999 and 2000 seasons, I could not even hit 10 rams, let alone go for a long run.

Wind on the Ridgway, Pennsylvania, silhouette range is tricky. Instead of being a crosswind or even a quartering wind, the wind on this range has a strong tendency toward being intermittent gusts of head and tail winds, that is, either 12 o'clock or 6 o'clock, and sometimes both at the same time on different parts of the range. To add to the problem, the firing line is located on a high rise of land, so bullets being directed toward

14

turkeys or rams are well over the treetops about 200 to 225 meters from the firing line. There are no wind flags up there!

The situation of intermittent gust head and tail winds results in a significant number of over and under shots on the rams. That is, with a dead center hold and sight setting, your shots can vary from over the back to dead center to under the belly all because of head and tail winds. It was with this situation in mind that in the fall of 1999 I began to think that possibly the extended length of the Postell bullet could make it more vulnerable to the wind. I based this on the fact my bullets were exiting the muzzle at 1,188 fps and had decelerated to about 889 fps at 550 yards. This also had to make a difference in the rotational velocity of the bullet at that range, though how much of a difference I had no idea. But whatever the difference, it had to result in some deterioration of stability of the long Postell bullet.

With this in mind I dug out my Dave Farmer nose-pour mould for the Lyman No. 457125 bullet. The height of the mould blocks was carefully measured and then the spacer between the cutoff plate and bottom plate was shortened so it measured only one and one-half thousandths (0.0015) inch greater than the height of the mould blocks. The spacer and plates were reassembled, making certain the plates were parallel their full length. This gave me bullets with absolutely perfect bases perpendicular to the axis of the bullet.

As mentioned earlier, this bullet is ⅛ inch shorter than the Postell bullet and weighs in at 528 grains when cast from an alloy that approximates 25-to-1 lead and tin. Bullets from my Steve Brooks Postell mould when cast of the same alloy weigh 540 grains.

These roundnose 457125 bullets from the readjusted Dave Farmer mould seemed to shoot equally as well as my favorite Postell bullets, and some of the test firing done on Brian Chilson's silhouette range indicated they just might give better performance on the rams.

I do not want to imply the Lyman roundnose 457125 bullet, or bullets of the same pattern from other moulds, is superior in performance to the old, original Postell design. Such is not necessarily the case. What I do imply is that the .45-70 cartridge case does not have sufficient powder capacity to drive the long, heavy Postell bullet at high enough muzzle velocity to assure positive stability of the bullet at the longer ranges. A velocity of 1,188 fps from a .45-70 case is a far cry from 1,350 fps with the same bullet from a .45x2.6 cartridge case!

The potential advantage of the shorter roundnose 528-grain bullet is twofold. One, at any given velocity, it is more stable than a longer bullet of the same weight; and two, because it is shorter, it does not seat as deeply in the cartridge case, thus providing an increase in powder capacity and muzzle velocity, which should also help stability at the longer ranges.

Now you can test bullets all you want at some local or private range, but the real test of a bullet is on the firing line in an approved shooting match where you are shooting against the clock and have no choice of weather conditions. Although after months of testing with the Dave Farmer 457125 bullet, during which time it seemed the bullet gave a slight edge in performance over my Postell, five consecutive silhouette matches proved otherwise with scores that were only one or two points below normal. So when I loaded ammunition for the Pennsylvania State Championship silhouette match for the year 2000, I went back to my Steve Brooks

Postell bullet sized to .455 inch diameter, 67 grains of GOEX FFg fired from a Federal premium cartridge case. Although my scores were not in the winner's circle, they were back where they belonged among the top 10 of some 50 odd shooters, and that is not bad for an OF who is nearing his 75th birthday!

The upshot of the whole thing is that I cannot seem to do better than the original design Postell bullet.

Since some may wonder why I switched from the Tom Ballard Postell to the Steve Brooks Postell, it is because the latter mould was purposely cut smaller over the driving bands so there is less sizing when the bullet goes through the sizing die. In addition, the Steve Brooks mould blocks are far heavier than the Lyman blocks used by Tom Ballard and do not warp as easily.

Although I used the Tom Ballard Postell bullet almost exclusively from March 12, 1995, through December 12, 1999, there were many other bullets I tried and then set aside for one reason or another. These were all superb bullets from excellent moulds, and the fact they did not give premium performance on a consistent basis in my rifle should in no way be taken as a general criticism of that bullet. In another rifle it may well outperform any bullet and load combination I could use in my rifle.

One of the most remarkable bullets in this respect is the RCBS 45-500-BPS. This is an excellent bullet weighing about 520 grains when cast 25-to-1 lead and tin and should not be overlooked by any shooter who is searching for a good production mould bullet. RCBS mould blocks rank among the very best of production moulds.

I first took this bullet to the Towanda Rifle and Pistol Club range on August 16, 1995. They were loaded in Remington cartridge cases in front of 67 grains of GOEX

FFg fired by Federal 215 primers. An eighty-thousandth (0.080) inch thick vinyl wad was used over the powder, and the bullet was lubed with my own lube. It was slightly foggy that morning with patches of fog drifting over the range, so shooting had to be done intermittently. It took me 5 to 10 minutes to fire five shots. Shooting was done at 300 yards, and when I brought the target in, the group measured just 2¾ inches center to center!

Naturally I was elated, especially so because just prior to firing that group I had tested another bullet on a full-size pig silhouette target and could barely keep the bullets on the pig.

The tough part of it was I never could get that bullet to approach that group size again. After three month's work with that bullet, during which time I fired several groups that hovered about 4½ inches center to center, I never could get the consistency in accuracy so necessary for silhouette shooting. I still believe the RCBS bullet is of superb design and that in another barrel would give superlative accuracy.

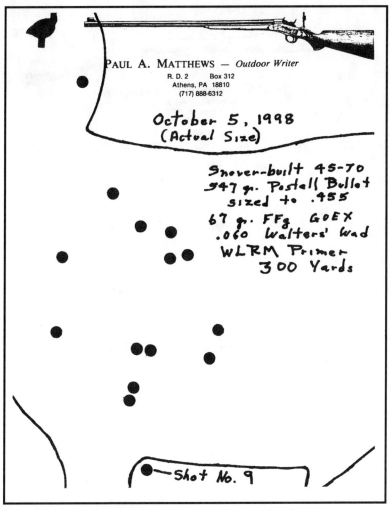

PAUL A. MATTHEWS — *Outdoor Writer*
R. D. 2   Box 312
Athens, PA 18810
(717) 888-6312

October 5, 1998
(Actual Size)

Snover-built 45-70
547 gr. Postell Bullet
sized to .455
67 gr. FFg GOEX
.060 Walters' Wad
WLRM Primer
300 Yards

●—Shot No. 9

Who says undersized bullets won't shoot? This group was fired at 300 yards on a reduced ram target using a Snover-built rolling block .45-70. The shot in the horn was the No. 1 shot. A sight adjustment was made after that shot and after shot No. 9. Fired October 5, 1998.

19

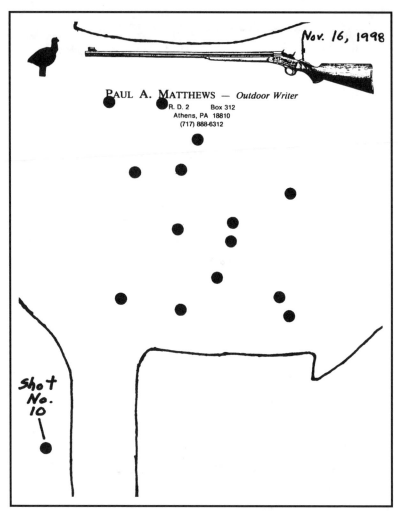

Nov. 16, 1998

PAUL A. MATTHEWS — *Outdoor Writer*
R. D. 2   Box 312
Athens, PA 18810
(717) 888-6312

Shot
No.
10

This is another group fired at 300 yards from a Snover-built rolling block using a 0.455 inch diameter original design Postell bullet weighing 550 grains. The load was 67 grains of GOEX FFg powder, 0.060 inch thick Walters vegetable fiber wad and Winchester WLRM primer. Sight adjustment made after shot No. 10.

3

Barrels and Chambers

I believe the rifle barrel is second in importance only to the chamber within that barrel. That is to say, I would rather have a premium chamber in a ho-hum barrel than to have a ho-hum chamber in a premium barrel. While I have never cut a chamber in my life, and wouldn't know how to begin the job of threading and fitting a barrel, and cannot in any way be considered a knowledgeable expert on the subject of chambers and barrels, I seldom hear any shooter discuss the subject beyond the statement of who made the barrel on his or her rifle. And if the discussion does go beyond the name of the barrel maker, it usually ends with the pitch of the rifling.

Believe me, there is a lot more to a rifle barrel than the name of the maker or the amount of twist to the rifling. There is far more to it than this scribe will ever know, but knowing what little bit I do know and putting it to work can save considerable time and money and give you an edge on accuracy.

First, there is no "best" barrel maker. If there were such a person, he or she would be so swamped with work that to meet customer demands the barrel maker would have to take shortcuts or rely on methods of machining that would make the final product no better than that of his competitors. So if you are contemplating a new barrel or a custom rifle with a barrel of your choice, your first job is to decide exactly what you want in a rifle barrel and then select a barrel maker who can and will deliver what you want.

When it comes to a barrel for the black powder cartridge rifle, my own preference has always been one made, fitted and chambered by Ron Snover of IXL Enterprises. I favor a Snover barrel because Ron has the capability of cutting one groove at a time, for any specified twist, at any specified depth and of almost any style rifling you might choose. While all this costs money and may or may not contribute favorably toward better accuracy, it does give the customer certain options not available from some other barrel makers.

This does not mean that barrels from other barrel makers are second rate or somehow inferior to a Snover barrel. Far from it. I have seen too many out-of-the-box Browning silhouette rifles sporting a Badger barrel that shot top scores to make an assertion like that. What I am saying is that if you want a barrel cut to your specifications you have to go to a barrel maker who has the equipment and expertise to cut such a barrel. Ron Snover is just such a man. While I will not say that Ron makes the best barrel in the country, I will say that no one makes a better barrel.

I personally favor an odd number of lands in a barrel because I believe that having a land opposite a groove instead of opposite another land results in less distortion of the bullet. While this is one of those theories that cannot be proven, it makes sense to me. And that is all that counts! Thus it was that when I ordered my first barrel (and rifle) from Ron Snover in July 1993, the specifications called for five lands with a pitch of one turn in 18 inches. This to be in a round tapered barrel 34 inches long.

In further discussion of the barrel with Ron, he simply said he would follow the old Remington style rifling with five lands that were slightly narrower than the grooves at a ratio of about 55 percent to 45 percent. That is, 55 percent of the bore area would be groove and 45 percent would be land.

At that time the ratio between land and groove width held absolutely no significance for me. And when Ron handed me the completed rolling block rifle in February 1994, it was the most beautiful rifle I had ever held in my hands. More than that, it shot as good as it looked, and I used it almost exclusively for all my silhouette shooting right up until June 2000, burning at least a case of powder – usually more – in it every year.

One of the first things I learned with that barrel was that the nose diameter of my bullets had to be at least three thousandths (0.003) inch smaller than the bore diameter, or about .447 inch, if I were to get the precise accuracy required for silhouette shooting.

This was contrary to the new silhouette bullet moulds being cut on a production basis at that time. It seemed everyone wanted their bullet to have a bore-riding nose, yet when one looked at drawings of bullets designed in the black-powder era, or measured bullets cast in moulds of the black-powder era, nose diameters ran much smaller than bore diameter – the diameter across the tops of the lands.

For example, a government manual drawing of the

M1882 .45-70-500 cartridge reproduced on page 129 of J.S. and Pat Wolf's fine book *Loading Cartridges for the Original .45-70 Springfield Rifle and Carbine* shows the diameter of the nose just ahead of the front driving band to be .447 inch tapering to .443 inch at a point .350 inch from the nose end of the bullet. Drawings of the 405-grain bullet also shown in this book on pages 124 and 125 indicate a maximum nose diameter of .445 inch just ahead of the front driving band.

As mentioned in the chapter "Observations of the Bullet," my own original design Postell bullet from a mould purchased in 1950 had a nose diameter of .443 inch just ahead of the front driving band, while a second original design Postell bullet sent to me by Bill Pace of Texas measured .441 inch diameter at this location. This is a bullet originally designed for long-range shooting with black powder. And if the bore diameter nose feature really contributed to accuracy, it seems that it would have been used here.

Conversely, we probably all know a number of excellent riflemen who are shooting top scores using bullets having a bore-riding nose. So what is it that makes the difference? Why should bullets having a bore-riding nose give superb accuracy for one shooter, while another shooter must use bullets that are a full three thousandths (0.003) inch smaller on the nose than the bore diameter of his barrel? What makes the difference?

One obvious thought is that the smaller diameter nose more easily accommodates the black-powder fouling left in the barrel from a previous shot. And while this may have been a consideration in the bullet designs of 1865 to 1900, I have some doubts about its effects one way or another. I say this because for years I put a damp patch through my barrel following each shot. Thus I had a clean barrel for every shot with absolutely no improvement in accuracy with bullets having a bore-riding nose. In fact, they did not shoot as well as bullets with a smaller nose diameter.

It is my belief that accuracy in a black powder cartridge rifle with a cast bullet having a bore-riding nose is more dependent upon the width of the lands to support the nose of the bullet than anything else. I base this upon an article written by Col. E.H. Harrison, first published in the March 1958 issue of the *American Rifleman* and later reprinted in a book *Cast Bullets* published by the National Rifle Association in 1979.

On page 25 of that book, Col. Harrison puts forth the premise that barrels having lands and grooves of equal width, or barrels having very wide lands, will usually give superb performance with cast bullets having a long bore-riding nose, whereas barrels having lands that are narrower than the grooves are at their best with bullets having a "groove-size body of good length."

Although the colonel was talking primarily about cast bullets for smokeless loads in high-powered rifles, and divides bullet selection between those with a long bore-riding nose and those with a long groove-size body, I believe his basic premise is correct. That is, I believe that if the lands in your barrel are narrower than the grooves, you will probably get your best accuracy with a bullet having a nose diameter at least three thousandths (0.003) inch smaller than the bore diameter of your barrel. If the lands and grooves in your barrel are of equal width, or if the lands are wider than the grooves, you will probably get your best accuracy with a bullet having a bore-riding nose.

This has all been borne out by actual practice in the three barrels Ron Snover has made, fitted and chambered for me. In each case the lands were narrower than the grooves, and in each case it was a bullet with a nose diameter at least three thousandths (0.003) inch smaller than the bore diameter that gave the best accuracy.

In the chapter "Observations of the Bullet" there was a lengthy discussion relative to the inside diameter of fireformed cartridge cases and its relevance to the driving band diameter of the cast bullet. If you missed that, you should go back and read it, because that all relates to the chamber and chamber dimensions.

What we have said about internal barrel dimensions and internal chamber and fireformed case dimensions should serve as a guide for your cast bullet dimensions. While in all probability most beginning silhouette shooters start with a production bullet mould – and this makes sense – somewhere along the line they realize they are capable of better accuracy than they are getting, and they start looking at different cast bullets. It is at this point I believe they should start looking at internal barrel and chamber dimensions and apply this information to the dimensions of their cast bullets.

Most barrels you see on black powder cartridge rifles have the same basic land and groove configuration regardless of whether the lands are the same width or narrower than the grooves, and regardless of the number of the lands and grooves involved. That is, a cross section or end view of most barrels will show a cross section of the lands to be shaped as small, slightly curved rectangles evenly spaced about the inside circumference of the barrel. This means the top of each land has two sharp outside corners, and the bottom of each land has two sharp inside corners, one on each side where the bottom of the land meets the groove.

Both the tops of the lands and the bottoms of the grooves are cut on a radius from the center of the bore, the radius or depth of the grooves usually being about four thousandths (0.004) inch. Over the years this land and groove configuration has proved to be very effective with lead alloy bullets. About the only factor that decreases the effectiveness of this configuration is shallow grooves, grooves that are only about half as deep. And this deterioration in effectiveness is limited to the grooved-lubricated or naked-lead alloy bullet. Paper patched bullets always shot well in the old Remington and Sharps rifles having shallow grooves, and metal jacketed bullets often give exceptional accuracy in Marlin Micro-Groove® rifling having very shallow grooves.

The downside of this sharp cornered land and groove configuration is that it readily collects and retains black-powder fouling, and sometimes gives severe leading problems with alloy bullets. While some of this may be the fault of the bullet lubricant being used and/or the composition of the bullet alloy, a large portion of the blame can be attributed to the sharp corners mentioned earlier. Black-powder fouling builds up on the inside corners where the bottoms of the lands meet the grooves, and it does not take too long for it to bake onto the surface of the bore in this location and to strip, gouge or otherwise disfigure every lead alloy bullet that passes down bore.

This problem of fouling in the black-powder rifle is aggravated by hot temperature and low humidity. Those who put a damp patch through their barrel after every shot – and I did it for years – have little or no problem keeping the barrel free of baked-on fouling, while those who use a blow tube to blow moisture laden air through the barrel to keep the fouling soft are sometimes doing a lot of huffing and puffing.

While I have used both methods to keep the barrel free of baked-on fouling, there is a different style of rifling that will do a lot toward reducing the problem, especially on hot, dry days.

Sometime after Ron Snover built my first rifle, I was in his shop at Lehighton, Pennsylvania, and he handed me a rifle he had just rebarreled. Looking through the bore I was amazed to see there were no sharp corners on the rifling. In fact, it looked like a barrel that had been fired and cleaned so much that all the sharp corners of the lands and grooves had been worn to the extent they no longer existed. In the mirror-like finish of the bore, you could see the tops of the lands and the pitch of the rifling, but not one single sharp corner! It was Metford rifling developed over a century ago for the express purpose of reducing fouling problems on hot, dry days while doing intense firing.

Metford rifling is a form of segmental rifling in which the grooves are cut as a segment of a circle beginning at the top of one land and extending to the top of an adjacent land. In a .45-caliber barrel having Metford rifling, there will be seven grooves, each groove being about four thousandths (0.004) inch deep and without a sharp corner anywhere to provide an attachment for black-powder fouling.

While a look through a bore with Metford rifling might give the impression there is little gripping surface of the lands with which to rotate the bullet, especially a very soft alloy, this has not been a problem with a 25-to-1 lead and tin alloy bullet in my .45-70. Nor has it

28

been a problem in the .50x2½ Sharps that Ron built for me or the Big Fifties he built for nephews Eric and Mark.

While Metford rifling may not be a cure-all for fouling problems on hot, dry days, it certainly is superior to the conventional rifling found in most barrels. A barrel with Metford rifling cleans much easier than the conventional type simply because you do not have the sharp inside corners that provide an attachment for black-powder fouling.

One day in late summer of 1997, I mentioned to my wife, Betty, that if I were younger, I would have a new silhouette rifle built and that it would incorporate several changes over the rolling block I was using at the time. Specifically, the barrel would be rifled in the Metford style, it would be 30 inches long as opposed to the 34-inch barrel on the rolling block, and it would be 1⅛ inch straight octagon with no taper as opposed to the round tapered barrel on the rolling block.

Unbeknown to me until a year and a half later, Betty wrote down all I said and ordered just such a rifle from Ron Snover. And, Ron, not wanting to take any chances on such a project, joined me for a day of silhouette rifle practice on Brian Chilson's private range at Nelson, Pennsylvania. During the course of shooting, Ron asked me what I would have if I were to build a new silhouette rifle. And without any inkling of what was going on, I repeated exactly what I had told Betty a few months earlier.

Now the departure from a 34-inch round tapered barrel to a 30-inch straight octagonal barrel is quite radical, but not without sound reason. Although my rolling block .45-70 with the longer barrel gave superb accuracy on a consistent basis, it had a habit of suddenly and unpredictably changing point of impact during a long string of shots. For example, if I had my shots centered on the pig silhouette and suddenly a shot struck on the hind leg – and I had not called that shot out – I had better make a sight adjustment or my next shot would be within 1.5 inches of the hind leg shot. That was as predictable as night follows day!

What caused the barrel to do that, I have no idea unless it was the changing of internal stresses within the barrel. But the change was totally unpredictable. It might be after five shots, or after 10 shots, or it might not happen at all. When it did happen, I always made a sight adjustment and seldom regretted it.

From this experience, I felt that a shorter, stiffer barrel would be more stable, and thus it was that when I outlined the specifications for a new silhouette rifle, I chose a 30-inch barrel over a longer one.

To further promote the stability of the barrel during long strings of shots, I specified a straight octagonal configuration 1⅛ inches across the flats. While this is strictly theory on my part and contrary to the opinion of many barrel makers, I believe that for a given length, weight and internal dimensions, an octagonal barrel has the potential for better accuracy than a round barrel. I believe this because from the instant of ignition until the bullet exits the muzzle – known as barrel time – the round barrel can vibrate in any one of 360 directions, whereas the octagonal barrel can vibrate in only 8 directions.

If you question this line of thought, grasp one end of an octagonal barrel in a vise and try to bend it across corners! With the application of a bit of barnyard physics, I believe it might be possible to reduce the vibrations of an octagonal barrel to two directions simply by milling two opposing flats sufficiently enough to get a thinner wall section than is in the rest of the barrel. Whether or not this would prove to be the case or what the resulting accuracy would be, I have no idea.

At any rate, when the new silhouette rifle finally arrived in February 1999, the shorter, stiffer octagonal barrel did prove to be more stable than the longer, tapered round barrel. Of course, this is not a fair comparison as the octagonal barrel was much heavier in actual weight than the round barrel.

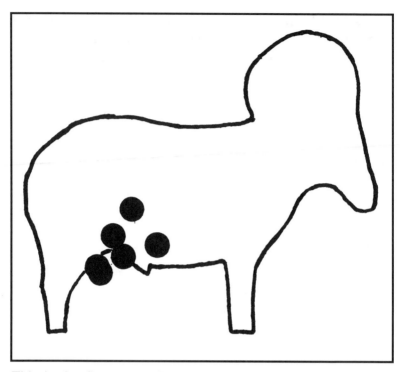

This is the first group fired from a new .45-70 rifle built by Ron Snover on a new Hepburn action by Oklahoma Territory Arms Company, LLC. The barrel is full octogon, 1⅛ inches across the flats, 30 inches long with 18-inch twist Metford rifling, fitted and chambered by Ron Snover. Sights were also made by Ron Snover.

The load was a 550-grain Ballard-Postell bullet sized 0.455 inch backed by 67 grains GOEX FFg powder, 0.060 inch thick Walters vegetable fiber wad, Winchester WLRM primer and Federal premium cartridge cases. Temperature was 28 degrees Fahrenheit. A blow tube was used between shots, and three sighter shots were taken before firing the group.

This group was fired by three different shooters, each taking two shots apiece with no sight adjustment. Shooters (in reverse order) were Ron Snover, Eric Matthews and Paul Matthews. Group measured 1³⁄₁₆ inches center to center. Fired February 20, 1999.

4

Shooting for a Group – How Good Is It?

For 50 years after I came home from World War II and started taking my shooting seriously, I did what all the gun writers of the day said I should do when testing my rifle and load for accuracy. I put up a target at 100 yards and fired 5 or 10 shots without any sight adjustment to see just how closely together the bullets would group on my target. It made sense to do this with a high-powered rifle, usually equipped with a scope sight. And when I started shooting competitively on the silhouettes with a black powder cartridge rifle, I continued the practice whenever testing or practicing on a bullseye target.

Even today when talking to other black powder cartridge rifle shooters, I am asked how close will my rifle group with this or that load on the pigs or rams or turkeys. When I tell them I quit shooting for groups in 1997, they look at me as if I have lost my marbles or am getting senile.

There is no question but what one can shoot excellent groups with no sight adjustment while using a black powder cartridge rifle. I have done it many times myself. But is it the right way to go? Can you really test a new load or bullet by shooting for a group at 300 yards? And if you get one or two off shots in the string, does it mean the load is unsatisfactory? Or does it mean there was a subtle change in light, mirage or wind that caused the off shots?

Think about it for a minute. When you are shooting at the silhouettes in competition, do you shoot at the entire bank of animals with no sight adjustments and no "Kentucky" windage? Or are you making minor adjustments to your sights or sight picture to compensate for all the natural changes going on between you and the target?

The most important feature of a good load is not whether it will fire a good group at 100 or 200 or even 300 yards, but whether or not that particular load will respond to sight adjustments and just how close that response is. That is, if you are shooting at a pig silhouette at 300 meters and your bullet strikes near the belly line, can you raise your sights half a minute or a quarter of a minute and have the next shot respond accordingly?

You have to remember that when you make a sight adjustment you are not correcting for a single bullet but for a group of bullets or a cone of fire. That is, for a load to be competitive it should stay at a maximum within two minutes angle of accuracy at the longest range at which you are shooting – this with sight adjustments or holding Kentucky. Thus, at 300 meters on the pigs, you should be able to control your bullets so they strike within a 6-inch area, leaving 2 to 3 inches above and below the strike area, depending upon where you are centered.

Going back to the hit that was near the belly line, if this hit was on the lower edge of your cone of fire and you raised your sight half a minute, your next shot could be on the upper edge of the cone of fire or about 1.5 to 2 inches above the horizontal centerline of the pig. And this is good – just so your bullets are striking near the horizontal center of your animal leaving some margin top and bottom for error, light changes, wind, etc.

Obviously, the smaller the strike area of your bullets, the more room you have to accommodate shots that wander outside the strike area for whatever reason. And it is these shots that usually tell you that you need a sight adjustment.

If you have done your part in casting quality bullets and loading quality ammunition, and you are confident of your sight picture and trigger squeeze, then you can be equally confident that when the bullet wanders outside the normal strike zone, it is because something between your eye and the target changed. Had that change not occurred, the bullet would have been within the normal strike zone. Knowing this, you can make a sight adjustment or a sight picture adjustment (Kentucky) and put your next shot within the normal strike zone.

I am certain many who read this will say that if you have a load that will give a good group, it will also respond to sight adjustments within the parameters of that adjustment and the cone of fire. This is true. I am not saying otherwise. What I am saying is that in order to get good groups with a specific load on a consistent basis with a given sight setting, *all conditions must be the same for every shot.* And in the world of the black powder cartridge rifle shooter, this almost never happens.

At any given distance, large diameter, heavy lead alloy bullets at black-powder velocities are far more vulnerable to wind, light change, mirage, etc. than are the smaller, lighter, high-velocity bullets from a high-powered rifle. This is strictly because of the longer time of flight over a given distance for the black powder cartridge rifle.

For example, as nearly as I can determine, my 540-grain Brooks-Postell bullet has a ballistic coefficient of .417 at the muzzle. At 1,188 fps muzzle velocity, it takes this bullet 0.54 second to travel 200 yards, and in a 10-mph wind it will be deflected 6.8 inches.

By comparison, the Sierra MatchKing 200-grain, .30-caliber bullet has a ballistic coefficient of .577. At 2,800 fps muzzle velocity, it reaches the 200-yard target in 0.22 second and is deflected 2.4 inches in a 10-mph wind.

If this 10-mph wind were constant in this example, one could correct for it and still shoot a good group. But in real life, the wind is seldom constant and may be but a strong gust somewhere between the muzzle and the target. Regardless of whether it is constant or merely a strong gust, the heavy Postell bullet is going to be deflected nearly three times as much as the Sierra bullet. This means that where the Sierra bullet might merely enlarge the group a bit, the Postell bullet will be out of the group sufficiently enough to make one believe it was an off shot due to some deficiency in the load rather than a single undetectable gust of wind 75 yards from the muzzle.

This is why I do not test bullets or loads by shooting for a group. There is just no way one can detect stray gusts of wind, subtle light changes or mirage with sufficient accuracy to determine the real cause of one or two bullets leaving the group. The important thing is to be able to control the bullet's point of impact by sight adjustment or a slight change in sight picture. If you can do that, you have a good load.

Before leaving this topic, I want to call your attention back to the comparison between the 540-grain Brooks-Postell bullet and the Sierra 200-grain MatchKing bullet. Note that this comparison was made *at a given distance of 200 yards and not for a given time of flight.* If we compare the same two bullets at the same muzzle velocities and *for a given time of flight,* the heavy Brooks-Postell bullet is far superior relative to wind drift even though the Sierra MatchKing has a much higher ballistic coefficient.

For example, our Brooks-Postell bullet required 0.54 seconds to travel 200 yards and was deflected 6.8 inches by a 10-mph wind. If we let the Sierra MatchKing bullet travel for 0.52 seconds (two hundredths [0.02] second less than the Brooks-Postell), it will have traveled 425 yards and will have been deflected 11.4 inches!

This simple observation tells us two things of significance to the black powder cartridge rifle shooter. One, the longer the bullet is exposed to the wind, the greater will be its deflection. And two, the bigger and heavier the bullet, the more nearly it will perform as though in a vacuum (or the less it will be deflected by the wind).

To get back to the subject of why shooting for a group with the black powder cartridge rifle can be extremely misleading, on August 2, 2000, my wife and I went to the Towanda Rifle and Pistol Club range to confirm the performance of a new load with two different bullets.

We had a bright afternoon sun in a cloudless sky and no apparent wind.

As usual, I was using a ram silhouette target on which the ram had been proportionately reduced for 300-yard shooting. For the first load, I was using a 540-grain Postell bullet cast in a Steve Brooks mould over a charge of 75 grains of GOEX Cartridge powder fired by a Winchester WLRM primer in a Winchester case. A damp patch was put through the barrel following each shot.

The first shot from the Hepburn .45-70 was high over the back, calling for a reduction of two minutes in elevation. The following nine shots made a nice round group on the ram 4⅞ inches center to center of the widest holes. One minor elevation change was made during the firing of the nine shots.

The second load was identical to the first except that the Postell bullet was replaced by a 529-grain copy of the Lyman 457125 bullet cast from a nose-pour mould made by Dave Farmer. Since I did not want any of these bullets to interfere with those I had just fired, I put four minutes left windage on the tang sight and continued to use the ram as the sighting point. The group fired is reproduced here. As you can see, shots numbers 2, 3 and 4 were each successively higher than the preceding shot due to some subtle light change taking place between shots. Following shot number 4, the rear sight was lowered half a minute placing the next six shots in the vicinity of shots numbers 1, 2 and 3.

Had I not lowered the sight after firing shot number 4, it is probable that at least one of the following shots would have been higher than shot number 4 and another farther to the right. As it is, the extreme spread of these shots measured from the center of number 4 is 6¼ inches, or a shade better than two minutes, whereas the extreme spread of all shots except number 4 is 4¹¹⁄₁₆ inches or a bit better than a minute and a half.

The point is that had I been shooting for a group with no sight adjustment as is the usual practice, and based my opinion of the load on those results, I would have classified it as a mediocre load at best and not suitable for competition.

While I know some will disagree with me – and that is their prerogative – you cannot accurately determine the true nature and performance of a load or bullet from a black powder cartridge rifle by firing a series of shots with no sight adjustment to determine how closely the shots will group together.

On the afternoon that I fired the foregoing group, there was no discernable light change from one shot to the next. Yet a quick glance at the target clearly indicates a definite change between shots 2 and 3, and again between shots 3 and 4.

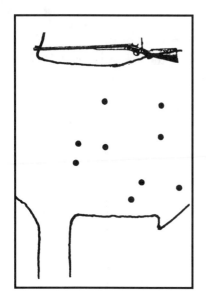

This group was fired at 300 yards on a reduced ram target with the Snover-built Hepburn .45-70. Load consisted of a 540-grain Brooks-Postell bullet cast 0.455 inch diameter, 75 grains of GOEX Cartridge powder, 0.030-inch Walters vegetable fiber wad, Winchester case and Winchester WLRM primer. Sight adjustments between shots made when necessary. A damp patch was put through the barrel following each shot. Group measured 4⅞ inches center to center. Fired August 2, 2000.

This group was fired at 300 yards with the Snover-built Hepburn. Load consisted of a 529-grain 457125 bullet cast in a Dave Farmer nose-pour mould, 75 grains of GOEX Cartridge powder, 0.030-inch Walters vegetable fiber wad, Winchester case and Winchester WLRM primer. A damp patch was put through the barrel after every shot. Following shot No. 4, a sight adjustment of one-half minute downward was made. The location of shots No. 1, 2, 3 and 4 indicates how a subtle change of light (or something) can enlarge a group when you attempt to shoot for a group without sight adjustment. Actual group size from center to center of shot No. 4 is 6³⁄₁₆ inches.

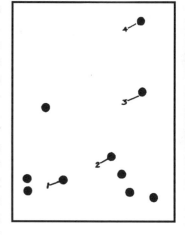

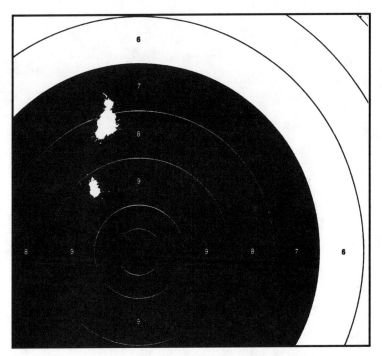

Here is another group that illustrates how a light change significantly affects the size of a group. This was fired at 100 yards by Ron Snover on August 24, 1996, using a Sharps-Borchardt rifle barreled and chambered by himself for the .45x2.6 cartridge. The load consisted of 94.5 grains of GOEX Cartridge powder and a 522-grain bullet from a Paul Jones mould. The lubricant was Matthews No. 1.

The interesting thing about this group is that the first two shots were fired during a bright sun and went into the upper group. Then a cloud covered the sun while Ron fired the next two shots that made the lower group. As soon as the sun broke through again, Ron fired two more shots that went back into the upper group. Extreme spread center to center is 1⅞ inches, but had all shots been fired under a bright sun, there is good evidence the extreme spread for all six shots would have been significantly less than an inch.

5

Light and Mirage – with a Transit

On the morning of July 23, 2000, I arrived at Brian Chilson's silhouette range a few minutes after 8:00. The sun was quarter high, and as I looked downrange, the swinger targets glistened with black dampness against a backdrop of plate steel painted tan. Just a few feet behind the firing position, a surveyor's transit was set up and aligned downrange.

As we moved my gear from the back of the vehicle to the firing position, I gave the transit little thought. But once we were set up and ready to shoot, we both went back and looked through the transit without touching it. The crosshair was centered precisely on the ram swinger right at the point of his ram hood with the ram facing to the right.

After 30 or 34 minutes of shooting, during which time I shot at the pigs and Brian shot at the turkeys, we again looked through the transit and were somewhat surprised to see that the rear foot of the ram now rested on the horizontal crosshair, and that within the span of two or three minutes the image of the ram had again shifted so that the horizontal crosshair was halfway up the rear leg and the crosshair had shifted a bit to the left.

We went back to our shooting, and after another 45 minutes checked the transit again. This time the crosshairs were halfway up the body of the ram. By the time we finished shooting at 11:30, the horizontal crosshair was resting on top of the ram's rump! This meant that from the time we first started shooting until the time we finished, the reflected image of the ram swinger had first shifted upward 5 inches and then had shifted downward 19 inches – all due to sun angle change or mirage or a combination of both. No wonder the rams are difficult to hit at 547 yards!

When I related this experience to another silhouette shooter, his response was, "I have a hard time accepting that." In short, he did not believe it.

The limits of my knowledge concerning light rays are restricted to a few basics. One, light rays are chaotic. That is, they go in all directions unless tunneled to go in one direction. Two, I learned in physics class some 60-odd years ago that the angle of reflection is equal to the angle of incidence. And three, probably the most important for silhouette shooters, light rays are easily bent by water or moisture in the air.

Yes, there is one other basic fact about light that is vitally important to the shooter. That is, that what we actually see as a target is the image of that target reflected back to us. That is, if a target or any other object does not reflect light, we would not see that target or object. And because it does reflect light, and that light is often reflected at an angle, and the reflected light rays are often bent by moisture in the air, and that moisture is often in motion, the reflected image of the target we see and shoot at is not always precisely where the target is. That is why we often miss a ram or turkey

44

with what we believe to be a perfect sight picture and perfect trigger control.

Shooters who have a difficult time grasping the fact the reflected image of a target has considerable movement due to changing light, mirage and wind should do the following simple experiment. Sit down at a table with an empty teacup in front of you. Put a bright penny in the bottom center of the cup. Now, while sitting straight in the chair, slowly push the cup away from you until you can no longer see the penny. While maintaining that position, have someone slowly pour cold water into the cup (slowly so as not to move the penny) and watch the penny come back into view even though you know it is hidden by the rim of the cup!

The thing that has happened here is that the light rays striking the penny and being reflected from the penny are drastically bent by the water so that you see the image of the penny where the penny isn't!

The same thing happens when you are shooting at the rams, and just before you let the shot off, the mirage starts boiling upward like steam from a cauldron. In those few seconds, the reflected image of the ram has moved upward and your sight picture with a dead center hold changed with it. Your shot will be just over the back of the real target.

Mirage is nothing more than light rays being distorted by moisture in the air and set in motion by whatever wind or breeze is present. Like the penny in the teacup, you can see the reflected image of the ram clear as day. But that is all it is, a reflected image that may or may not be precisely where the real target is.

With all that said, let's go to an article that discusses mirage and light that appeared in the January 1991 issue of *Shooting Sports USA*. Titled "Understanding Mirage and Light" written by Glen Zediker, the author states in the second paragraph as follows: "The effect of mirage on your sighting, though, really can't be accurately compensated for. To skip the gist of this article: the basic advice is to shoot through the mirage to the center of the aiming black, no matter where it appears to be."

In order to keep that statement in context, you have to understand this article was directed at high-powered rifle shooters using rifles equipped with iron sights but firing high-velocity cartridges loaded with smokeless powder and match grade metal jacketed bullets. And while one has to believe that under these conditions the advice given in the quoted paragraph is 100 percent correct, one also has to question the application of this advice for the black powder cartridge rifle silhouette shooter who is using a low-velocity, high-trajectory cartridge to drive a less-than-perfect bullet through a rifle barrel fouled by black powder from a previous shot.

Let's face reality. If you are shooting at the rams 547 yards distant under absolutely perfect conditions with a perfect sight picture and perfect trigger control for each shot, and you have a good load in a good rifle, you are doing good shooting if you can stay within minute and a half angle of accuracy. At that distance, a minute and a half amounts to a shade over 8 inches, and with the body of the ram averaging a shade over 12 inches from back line to belly line, you have a margin for error of only 2 inches above or below your 8-inch group or cone of fire.

Now, let's assume you have sighted in on the swinger with a dead center hold and little perceptible mirage. You take a similar sight picture on your first ram for score, but just before you apply the final bit of pressure to the trigger, the mirage starts to boil furiously off the top of the ram. Without any conscious knowledge on your part, the reflected image of the ram has shifted upwards, and if your shot is near the upper edge of your group or cone of fire, it will be over the back of your target.

Now, let's assume that to compensate for this near miss, you lower your sight half a minute and go on to ram No. 2. For this shot, the boil completely disappears and, according to Murphy's Law, the shot is on the bottom edge of your group or cone of fire. Again, you miss your target, only this time it is under the belly.

If you consider these two hypothetical shots as described, then you may be inclined to agree with Mr. Zediker that one is better off to shoot through the mirage at the center of the target with no sight adjustment or Kentucky. But if you have a spotter who keeps you informed of the direction and characteristics of the mirage, and you keep in mind the conditions of the mirage when you fired your sighter shots, then you can compensate for the mirage by holding a shade high or low as required on successive rams.

Why try to hold dead center on a target squirming with mirage when you know from our experiment with the transit that the image of the target can and does shift several inches in changing light conditions, some of which may well be mirage related?

Later on in his article, Mr. Zediker states that these high shots are more likely to be the result of updrafts that are causing the boil rather than the boil itself. Even if this is a correct analysis of the situation, one is still better off to compensate for an updraft indicated by a boiling mirage than to ignore the mirage and try to shoot through it. Believe me, top black powder cartridge rifle shooters are top shooters because they compensate for wind, mirage, light conditions or whatever, not because they ignore them. One cannot ignore the fact that the angle of light striking the target, the intensity of that light, the angle of the target relative to the shooter and the degree of perceptible mirage all have a profound influence on how and where the target appears to the shooter.

How many of us during a day of competition have noticed that one specific animal within a particular bank of targets seemed to be subject to more misses than normal, especially when all the other animals on the bank were struck with systematic regularity? And how many of us upon noticing this have later checked that specific animal to see if there was a difference between it and its neighbors?

Animals that get hammered by the high-powered rifle shooters sometimes get distorted in shape so they reflect light at a radically different angle than their neighbors and thus are not exactly where they appear to be. While it may be difficult and even unwise to claim this is absolutely and positively the cause of a miss, I recall only too well missing the No. 4 pig twice in a row on a day when I had no problem with all the others. The next morning while setting targets for pre-match practice, I noticed the body of No. 4 pig had been hammered by bullets until it was no longer flat like its neighbors but was appreciably concaved. There is no way this pig would reflect light in the same direction as the other pigs on the same bank, and I firmly believe this was the cause of my two misses. And I believe it happens more than we realize with the turkeys, not be-

48

cause they are deformed or distorted in shape, but because of the slight difference in angle at which they are placed on the rail. Change the angle at which the sun strikes the target and you have changed the angle at which the sun is reflected from that target!

Getting back once more to the shifting of the target image due to mirage, and the article by Mr. Zediker, there is a statement in the article that says, "Surveyors, who deal a lot more with mirage than shooters do, will steadfastly say that mirage does not actually cause an object to relocate; they aim right at the center of the object they're referencing to without compensating for the distortion of mirage."

While I am in no position to say this conclusion is in error, I am in a position as one seeking knowledge to pose a question relative to this conclusion, especially in view of Brian Chilson's and my experience with the transit on the firing line. Although my experience at surveying is limited to helping a county surveyor map out a couple farms, and watching surveyors at work on various construction locations, I have to ask just how often does a surveyor take a bearing on an object 547 yards away? And when he does take such a bearing, how important or critical is 2½ inches? On those jobs where even one inch might be critical, just how far away from the object is the transit? And how long is the transit crosshair centered on the referenced object before moving to the next?

After having missed more than my share of rams with over and under shots, some due to wind and some due to mirage, and after having witnessed first-hand that the reflected image of an object does indeed relocate due to light changes, angle of reflection and/or just

49

plain old mirage, I am not about to shrug my shoulders and ignore the facts and try to shoot through it.

While I will never be the equal of many of the top shooters in this black powder cartridge silhouette game, you can bet your last primer that when my spotter tells me the mirage is boiling off the tops of the rams, I'll shade my shot a bit low. And when my spotter tells me the mirage is streaking left or right when on the last shot it was subdued, you can bet I will use a bit of left or right Kentucky to compensate.

6

How to Make a High-Capacity Casting Dipper

Casting lead alloy bullets for competitive shooting in the black powder cartridge rifle is a different ball game from that of casting bullets for casual shooting. It demands the very best of casting skills and equipment, and among the items of equipment most often over-looked is the dipper with which we pour the molten alloy. Yes, I realize there are those who use a bottom-pour melting pot, but most who are casting the heavy, large-caliber bullets for black powder cartridge rifle competition use the old cast iron dipper offered by Lyman or RCBS.

Each of these dippers is an excellent product. Lyman's has been on the market since the late 1800s and was redesigned only a few years ago. The RCBS dipper has been on the market for longer than many shooters today have been on the range. But in the casting of pre-mium bullets for the black powder cartridge rifle, par-ticularly heavy, large-caliber bullets in a nose-pour mould from an alloy having a high casting temperature, a large-capacity dipper is needed to provide sufficient weight to assure complete fill-out of the mould before the metal starts to harden.

Not only do we need the backup weight of molten alloy within the dipper, we also need a nozzle on the dipper that has a large pour hole and that seats in the bottom of the beveled recess in the cutoff plate. This allows the alloy to flow directly into the mould cavity with little or no cooling off contact with the cutoff plate.

I should point out that just because a dipper or ladle holds more bullet metal, that in itself does not mean the weight behind the bullet as it is poured into the mould is any greater than that from a ladle of lesser capacity. The actual weight behind the bullet as it is poured into the mould from a dipper with the bowl held in a vertical position is equal to the weight of a column of bullet metal extending from the hole in the cutoff plate to the surface of the molten metal in the bowl, and no larger in diameter than the smallest orifice through which the metal must flow, be it the hole in the nozzle of the dipper or the hole in the cutoff plate.

Once you have that bit of information digested, then it becomes obvious that to make a superior dipper, that dipper must be designed to hold sufficient alloy so that when the dipper is turned vertical to put the weight of the metal within the dipper against that within the mould, the surface level of the metal within the dipper, measured from the end of the nozzle, must be greater than that of commercially available dippers. With the dipper described in this chapter, that dimension is about 1½ inches. The corresponding dimension on a new Lyman dipper is about 1³⁄₁₆ inches.

Although there are probably different ways to make a dipper that meets the criteria of the black powder cartridge rifle shooter, the method used by my old friend Charlie Canoll I believe is the best. With reference to the dimension drawing shown at the end of this section, we will go through the process on a step-by-step basis.

1. Obtain a short length of 1-inch galvanized pipe and face off both ends to a length of 1⅝ inches.

2. Using a piece of ⅛ inch thick steel stock about 2 inches square, weld this to one end of the length of pipe.

3. Grasp the length of pipe in a three-jaw chuck and machine the end plate down to the circumference of the pipe.

4. Using a second piece of ⅛ inch thick steel stock, weld the second end plate to the other end of the section of pipe and machine it down to the circumference of the pipe.

5. Stand the semi-finished bowl on one end and mark the location for the nozzle as shown on the drawing on one end plate. Drill through the end plate at this location with a ¹⁷⁄₆₄ inch diameter drill.

6. Clamp the semi-finished bowl in a milling machine making certain the hole for the nozzle is at top dead center. Cut away a portion of the bowl as shown in the drawing.

7. Using a piece of soft, non-hardened steel, machine a nozzle as shown in the drawing, paying particular attention to the .265 inch diameter. Ideally, this should be a snug friction fit with the hole in the end plate.

8. Using a standard flathead screw countersink, countersink the *inside* lip of the hole that you drilled through the end plate.

53

9. Now, take a piece of aluminum or steel stock that is ⅜ to ½ inch thick and about 1 inch wide. Length is unimportant. Grasp this piece of stock in a vise and drill a hole through it using a No. 29 drill. Tap this hole with a No. 8-32 thread tap and leave the piece in the vise.

10. Insert the short pilot end of the nozzle into the hole in the end plate of the bowl.

11. Using a 1 inch long No. 8-32 thread flathead screw, insert the screw into the hole in the nozzle from the inside of the bowl. Tip the bowl upright and thread the end of the screw into the tapped hole in the piece held in the vise.

12. Tighten the screw as tightly as you can get it to flare the inside of the nozzle into the countersink recess on the inside surface of the end plate. When properly done, the nozzle will be firmly and permanently secured to the bowl.

13. Using a piece of ½ inch round steel stock, make a handle socket as shown in the drawing.

14. Weld one end of the handle socket on the left horizontal centerline of the bowl, ¹³⁄₁₆ inch back from the front face of the bowl.

15. Use a piece of ⁵⁄₁₆ inch diameter steel dowel about 10 inches long and threaded ⁵⁄₁₆-18 thread on one end for a handle.

16. Make certain all the zinc galvanizing is burnt off the bowl *before* placing the dipper in a pot of molten metal. Zinc will contaminate a lead alloy and the melting pot it is in.

I have used a dipper made exactly as described for the past year for casting .45-caliber bullets up to 550 grains in both nose-pour and base-pour moulds. This dipper holds more alloy than either the Lyman or RCBS dippers and does a superb job of assuring a well filled out bullet when the casting temperature is up to what it should be.

The large hole in the nozzle gets the alloy into the mould in a hurry, and the slimness of the nozzle lets you place the tip of the nozzle in the bottom of the cavity in the cutoff plate.

Obviously you can modify the dimensions or materials described to obtain a larger dipper if deemed necessary. This might include using a short length of 1¼ inch diameter stainless steel tubing instead of the galvanized pipe. But whatever your choice, this is the best dipper I have ever used.

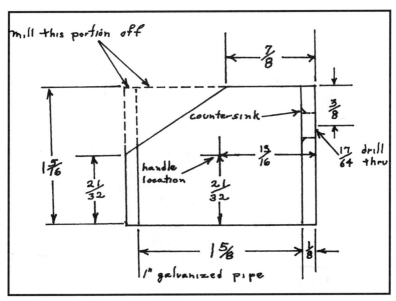

This is the bowl for the high-capacity casting dipper.

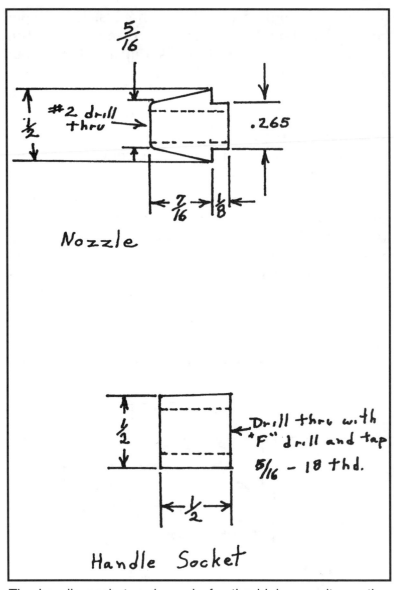

The handle socket and nozzle for the high-capacity casting dipper.

7

Primer Wads
– How Good Are They?

Primer wads are not new. I have been told that primer wads made of cigarette paper were often used by competitive shooters in the early 1900s, though I must confess that the first time I ever heard of them was in an article that appeared in a past issue of *The Black Powder Cartridge News*.

Perhaps the term primer wad is a bit misleading, because in this black powder cartridge rifle game, the term "wad" evokes an image of a thick disk cut from a milk carton, tablet back, low-density polyethylene, etc. Whatever the case, when we think of a wad, we normally visualize a disk ranging in thickness from twenty to sixty thousandths (0.020 to 0.060) inch to be placed over the powder for the purpose of protecting the base of the bullet and to help seal the bore against escaping powder gases.

By contrast, the primer wad is a disk cut from a thin sheet of paper or other material and placed between the primer and the powder. From what little experience I have had with primer wads, their function is to provide a more uniform ignition of the powder by creating a uniform barrier through which the primer flame must pass before igniting the powder. I am convinced this uniformity process does occur, and later I will give you the evidence to support this belief.

Primer wads can be positioned in one of two places: immediately under the primer or inside the cartridge case at the bottom of the powder column. At this stage of the game, I have no conclusion as to which location provides the superior performance or if one location is superior to the other. What I do know is that right now it seems to be much easier to place a disk of paper inside the cartridge case before applying the powder charge than to place a disk of paper in the bottom of the primer pocket prior to or during the primer seating operation.

When I first started working with primer wads in my .45-70, my inclination was to cut .45-caliber disks from the local newspaper using one of Fred Cornell's superbly designed and crafted wad cutters. But trying to manipulate a .45-caliber disk of newsprint into the bottom of a .45-caliber cartridge case that tapers to something less than .45 caliber as you get closer to the bottom of the cartridge case is a tricky, nuisance operation. The .45-caliber disk always reaches the bottom of the case in an on-edge position, and you play havoc trying to make it lie flat.

If you are going to place a primer wad in the bottom of the cartridge case, use a subcaliber wad and merely drop it in the mouth of an upright case. It will fall flat all by itself. For .45-caliber cases, use .38-caliber disks and for the .50 calibers, use a .45-caliber disk. I expect the .38-caliber disks would also work fine in any .40-caliber cartridge cases.

If you elect to place the primer wad under the primer, then you are limited in the thickness of the wad or disk of paper because the primer *must* be seated flush with or below flush with the face of the rim, and you must not crush the primer or distort it to obtain the proper seating depth.

Cutting thin disks of paper with a wad cutter calls for a very close fit of the cutting edges. Otherwise the wad will cut clean on most of its circumference, but will be left hanging in one spot – a frustrating nuisance. They must cut clean all the way around.

One of the worst materials for cutting clean is aluminum foil – yes, good, old Reynolds Wrap® aluminum foil that is only one and one-half thousandths (0.0015) inch thick! To cut this stuff clean, you must have a good, well-fitted wad cutter or else cut the disk with the primer during the primer seating operation.

This method of cutting disks to be placed under the primer is probably one of the best and most positive ways of doing the job. If you cut your disk as the primer is seated, then you are certain of getting only one thickness of disk material under the primer. Whereas if you place a precut disk in the bottom of the primer pocket prior to seating the primer, it is easy to pick up two disks that are stuck together and thus double the thickness of your primer wad. This, of course, would defeat the purpose and function of the primer wad.

Cutting the primer wad as you seat the primer can be a tricky operation depending upon the primer seating tool that you use. I have used an RCBS bench priming tool for years, except that I do not use the primer tube feed system, but place the primers in the priming rod one at a time by hand. This is an excellent priming tool

59

and is easily adaptable for cutting and seating the primer wad and primer in one operation.

In order to cut and seat a primer wad during the primer seating operation with the RCBS bench priming tool, you first place a primer in the top of the priming rod. Then you lift the handle to lower the priming rod, and with your other two hands slip the end of a $\frac{7}{16}$ inch wide strip of wad material into the top of the shellholder across the priming rod hole, and then slip in the cartridge case. A push on the handle cuts a clean wad or disk and seats the primer at the same time.

Only one problem here – we do not have three hands! To get around this problem, I drilled a $\frac{5}{16}$-inch hole through the base of my priming tool directly under the notch that is in the handle just ahead of the pivot screw. A .5-inch hole was then drilled down through the top of the bench with both holes aligned so a weight could be suspended from the notch in the handle. The weight is just heavy enough to hold the handle in the lifted position, making it easy to insert the wad material and cartridge case before seating the primer and wad.

As stated earlier, I have not experimented enough with primer wads to come to any conclusion as to where the wad should be located – under the primer or inside the cartridge case – or as to the best material to be used or its thickness. The field is wide open for experimentation.

Of the materials I have used, I can suggest that if you choose a thin paper such as 9-pound onionskin, make certain the paper has a uniform density. You can easily check this by looking through a sheet of paper held up to the light. Some papers made with 25 percent rag content will show a mixture of light and dark areas, while those made with 100 percent rag content will show an even opaqueness throughout. If you are using Reynolds Wrap aluminum foil, then you have just about the ultimate in uniformity of thickness and density. Why aluminum foil? Because it was suggested to me as coming from someone who should know that aluminum foil is the best material for primer wads. Whether or not this will prove to be the case remains to be learned.

Awhile back I wrote that I believed the primer wad helped to provide a more uniform ignition. The evidence that brought me to this conclusion occurred when I deburred the flash holes in 600 .50-90 cartridge cases by putting my Lyman deburring tool in an electric drill and giving each flash hole a short burst of power. I had done hundreds of other cartridge cases this way with no problem and saw no reason to anticipate a problem with the .50-90 cases.

However, where most cartridge cases have a healthy web thickness of .090 inch, the .50-90 cases, as we later found out, had a web thickness of only .060 inch. While this is more than adequate for the intended purpose of the cartridge case, the short burst of powder on the electric drill was sufficient to bevel the inside of the flash hole to a sharp edge at the bottom of the primer pocket. After four or five firings, the flash holes had eroded to the extent they were well oversize and of all different sizes. Accuracy from ammunition loaded with these cases went on vacation.

Not wanting to scrap 600 cartridge cases that we had paid dearly for, we cut some primer wads from newsprint using a .45-caliber Fred Cornell wad cutter. These wads were three thousandths (0.003) inch thick, and one wad was placed inside each cartridge case at the bottom of the powder column. Surprisingly, accuracy was restored to the same level as when the cases were new.

From this one incident, I have to believe the primer wad promotes a more uniform ignition. How much it will help in cartridge cases that have not been mutilated by an overly rambunctious uncle wielding an electric drill, I do not know. But the evidence is there. Primer wads do affect ignition.

After having written all that you have read so far, I loaded 10 cartridges using Federal Premium cartridge cases, Winchester WLRM primers, 67 grains of GOEX FFg, a 0.060 inch thick Walters vegetable fiber wad and a 540-grain bullet cast in my Steve Brooks Postell mould. The primers were all seated with a Reynolds Wrap aluminum foil primer wad underneath.

After using the first shot to foul the barrel, the other nine shots were fired over a Chrony chronograph with the following results:

1. 1,092 fps
2. 1,089 fps
3. 1,091 fps
4. 1,083 fps
5. 1,097 fps
6. 1,085 fps
7. 1,095 fps
8. 1,096 fps
9. 1,091 fps

Extreme spread – 14 fps
Average velocity – 1,091 fps
Standard deviation – 4.75 fps

I then compared these figures with those from an earlier test using the exact same load but without a primer wad. The results of this test were as follows:

1. 1,102 fps
2. 1,102 fps
3. 1,107 fps
4. 1,114 fps
5. 1,106 fps

Extreme spread – 12 fps
Average velocity – 1,106 fps
Standard deviation – 4.92 fps

While there are no significant differences in the results of the two tests, the velocity of shot No. 4 in the second listing was a spike, whereas there is no such spike in the first listing even though the velocity spread is 2 fps greater. In the first listing, that which used the primer wads, the velocities are more evenly spread out among the nine shots than in the second listing where no primer wad was used. The first listing, even though it has a slightly larger velocity spread, has a slightly smaller standard deviation.

You will also note there is a 15-fps drop in average muzzle velocity when using the primer wad, but whether the difference is due to the primer wad or difference in temperature or combination of both is questionable. The test figures for those cartridges without the primer wad were taken on July 16, 2000, with temperatures in the 80s, while those with the primer wad were taken on September 27, 2000, with temperatures in the 50s.

This temperature difference cannot be overlooked. Most black powder cartridge rifle shooters are well aware of the fact that in cold weather we have to raise our sights by two or three minutes or more for any given distance. To be meaningful, the tests should be run on the same day under the same conditions with the same number of shots for each test.

Although these test are extremely limited and inconclusive, they do give some indication that primer wads might promote more uniform ignition even in premium cartridge cases.

For the benefit of those who wish to conduct their own tests and calculate the standard deviation from those tests, following is the procedure I used, based on the figures listed for the second test.

1. Add the column of velocities.

$$
\begin{array}{r}
1,102 \\
1,102 \\
1,107 \\
1,114 \\
\underline{1,106} \\
5,531
\end{array}
$$

2. Divide the sum of the velocities by the number of individual velocities to obtain the average.

$$5,531 \div 5 = 1,106.2$$

3. Calculate the difference between each actual velocity and the average velocity.

$$1,102 - 1,106 = 4$$
$$1,102 - 1,106 = 4$$
$$1,107 - 1,106 = 1$$
$$1,114 - 1,106 = 8$$
$$1,106 - 1,106 = 0$$

4. Square each difference listed in step 3.

$$4^2 = 16$$
$$4^2 = 16$$
$$1^2 = 1$$
$$8^2 = 64$$
$$0^2 = 0$$

5. Add the squared differences determined in step 4.

$$\begin{array}{r} 16 \\ 16 \\ 1 \\ 64 \\ \underline{0} \\ 97 \end{array}$$

6. Divide the sum of the squared differences by the number of the original velocity figures *minus* one. Since we originally had five velocity figures, we will divide 97 by 4.

$$97 \div 4 = 24.25$$

7. Standard deviation is the square root of the answer determined in step 6, or in this case the square root of 24.25 is 4.924 as determined by pressing the square root button on my pocket calculator.

8

Powder Compression
– How Much?

Compressing the powder column is a vital operation when loading black-powder cartridges. Yet despite this, or perhaps because of it, there is no hard and fast formula one can apply with the certainty of success. Claims have been made that GOEX Cartridge powder responds well to heavy compression, while still others have advised me to limit the compression of GOEX Cartridge to somewhere between sixty (0.060) and one hundred thousandths (0.100) inch. And then there is also the advice that when loading some of the early lots of GOEX Cartridge manufactured in the Louisiana plant, compression should be below one hundred thousandths (0.100) inch or more than three hundred thousandths (0.300) inch. Anything in between is in the Twilight Zone.

Many years ago I read the quality of the performance of black powder is dictated primarily by how finely the components – potassium nitrate, charcoal and sulphur – are ground prior to mixing and formulation of the final product. While uniformity of granulation and amount of glazing also contribute to performance, without finely ground components the powder will not be of the highest quality regardless of other contributing factors.

If we accept this as fact, and I see no reason to do otherwise, then we come to the conclusion that if the components of a certain lot of powder were not properly ground, no amount of compression or lack of compression is going to make that particular lot of powder perform as well as another lot in which the components were properly ground.

With any given lot and granulation of powder, I believe there is a definite minimum and maximum point of compression. With the minimum point being that of 100 percent loading density with no compression at all, the maximum point is that to which you can compress the powder *without* fracturing the kernels in the powder column.

Once you start fracturing kernels, you no longer have the charge you started with; you have something else. For example, a particular lot of GOEX FFg made in May 1999 was giving me fits in the accuracy department when using the same charge, compression, bullet, etc. as used with a previous lot of the same powder. After shooting my lowest score in five years with this powder, I carefully pulled the bullets and withdrew the wads to examine the powder charge. Instead of finding 67 grains of FFg under the wad, I now had 67 grains of a mixture of dust, FFFFg, FFFg and FFg! There is no way, except by Providence, you can get consistent ignition with a load like that, and there is no way to control the fracturing of the kernels when compressing the powder charge in excess of the kernel strength. This powder was soft, too soft, and no manipulation of the load or change in compression would give me the accuracy of a previous lot manufactured in Moosic, Pennsylvania.

With that said, it becomes obvious that hard, well-glazed powders can be compressed more without fracturing the kernels than softer, not-so-well-glazed powders. And with this being true, the smart reloader will compress his powder somewhere within the limits of the strength of that powder and not in accordance with a magic number.

If, by some stroke of circumstance, I was getting superlative accuracy by compressing the powder charge well beyond the fracturing limit of the individual kernels, I would certainly continue to do so until I could find a better way of doing the job. There is absolutely no question but what a certain amount of compression to a given powder charge will often improve the burning characteristics of that powder charge with a resultant increase in velocity and a decrease in the amount of fouling. There is also little doubt in my mind that once you start fracturing kernels of the powder charge by excessive compression, you also increase the velocity spread.

In my opinion, the optimum amount of powder compression is a matter of common sense and experimentation. If the powder in our old government cartridges and many commercially loaded cartridges was compressed to a mixture of dust and all the intervening kernel sizes, it was for some reason other than superlative accuracy at the longer ranges.

It is not within the realm of common sense to compress a charge of black powder to the point where it becomes a mixture of dust and various other granulations. To do so is to ignore the very reason the powder was screened and graded during manufacture, and while one may get accuracy acceptable for military purposes or for the occasional hunter/shooter, you will not get accuracy consistently acceptable to the competitive shooter.

Anyone who has been in BPCR competitive shooting for any length of time knows that sometimes with some rifles some shooters once in awhile defy all logic and get excellent scores in doing so. While one cannot argue with success, one can say that staying within the parameters of logic and common sense relative to compression of the powder charge will get you more targets in more matches than will total disregard of such logic and common sense.

If we study some of the instructions for loading blackpowder cartridges as given to us in books and catalogs of yesteryear, there is almost always one item of advice common throughout regardless of how the compression is done or even if it is done. That piece of advice is to *never* crush the powder. In the old *Ideal Hand Book No. 4* (reprinted in the *Lyman Ideal Hand Book No. 39*), the final instructions in charging the shells state: "The powder should be packed, but never crushed, and should always receive the same pressure to insure regular and accurate shooting."

Again in an old Sharps catalog, the instructions for loading long-range cartridges read in part: "Place the shell in position and pour the powder slowly enough (through a 30-inch drop tube) to have it pack at least $\frac{1}{16}$ of an inch from the mouth of the shell. Over it put a thin wad of draughting [sic] paper and place the bullet within the shell with the fingers, making sure you do not tear the paper patch. Now place the ball-seater over it and press the ball gently down to the powder, and the cartridge is complete. Different batches of powder of the same brand often vary, so that it is found impossible to get in one hundred grains; in such a case use one to three grains less, as may be found necessary taking care not to crush the powder."

Note that in the Sharps instructions, the powder was not compressed at all, but merely packed by use of a 30-inch drop tube. Many years ago I watched Jerry Matalavage break down an original .40-70 Sharps straight cartridge loaded with a paper patched bullet (330 grains, if memory serves me correctly) and a thin green card wad over the powder. The powder charge had not been compressed and was just as bright and shiny as the day it was loaded. It weighed exactly 70 grains and poured from the cartridge case with no help from a screwdriver or other instrument.

Despite evidence from the past that advises us not to compress the powder to the extent of fracturing kernels, such advice is often ignored with superlative results. When I first started shooting in the BPCR silhouette matches at Wilton, New York, there were two outstanding gentlemen who, more often than not, held the winning score of the match. One of these shooters used a Hepburn .38-55 while the other used a Hepburn .45-70. Both were and are today excellent riflemen.

The ammunition used in the .38-55 was a bit unique in that the powder charge was what amounted to a full case of GOEX Fg compressed .5 inch to permit seating a fairly long, heavy bullet. Although such heavy compression in a target load was contrary to everything I had read on the subject, there was no getting around the fact the load was extremely accurate, and in 10 years of shooting at Wilton, I have never seen it fail to lay the rams flat on their backs following a full-bullet hit.

After watching the performance of this .38-55 load for a few matches, I had Fred Cornell make a pair of mould blocks with a simple ⅜ inch diameter cavity the same depth as the inside of a .38-55 Winchester cartridge case. Clamping the blocks together with a heavy C-clamp, the cavity was filled with GOEX Fg duplicating the load used at Wilton, and then compressed exactly ½ inch.

When the blocks were separated, I had a solid plug of powder that I could hold in my hand. But where I expected the plug to be nothing but crushed powder from end to end, such was not the case. Although the end of the plug that had been adjacent to the compression foot was crushed and compressed to a fine dust, from there on back the powder kernels became successively larger until at least the rear half of the plug was in its original Fg configuration. In short, here was a powder charge in which half of it was a successive layered mixture of dust, FFFFg, FFFg and FFg with the remainder of it being Fg. Why should such a powder charge give any semblance of accuracy?

The only theory I could possibly give to explain the favorable performance of this load is that it is a mechanically produced duplex load that apparently can be duplicated time after time with good uniformity. While the various granulations of powder seemed to be placed in the cartridge case in the reverse order of most duplex loads – that is, the slowest burning powder is next to the primer while the fastest burning is adjacent to the bullet – such an order is not without its potential. Many attempts have been made in the past toward a perforated powder charge that would permit the primer flame to ignite the front of the powder charge simultaneously with the rear so the powder column would not be driven partially up the barrel to spew burning embers out the muzzle, but would be totally consumed within the barrel.

Whether or not this theory is correct, and whether or not it would be applicable on a regular basis for various rifles and cartridges, remains to be seen. What is apparent is that sometimes excessive powder compression does result in a very accurate load.

There are other instances in which what appears to be excessive powder compression is not always such. I am speaking here of those shooters who double compress a charge in order to get 85 or 90 grains of powder in a .45-70 cartridge case. In such instances, half the powder charge is first put into the case and then compressed, followed by the other half of the powder charge and a second compression.

Whether or not this would qualify as excessive compression would depend upon how much each half-charge was compressed. Since the chamber on my own Snover-built .45-70 is throated to accept two driving bands and two grease grooves, my tapered bullet (Lyman No. 457675) weighing 513 grains is seated only 0.150 inch into the cartridge case. Using Winchester cartridge cases allows a charge of 85 grains of GOEX Cartridge, a 0.060 inch thick wad and 0.1 inch compression. And here the amount of compression could be reduced by using a thinner wad or no wad at all.

As stated earlier, the compression of the black powder charge is perhaps the most critical operation in the loading of a cartridge to be used in competition. While a degree of compression will almost always give a slight increase in velocity with less fouling, if you vary the amount of compression from cartridge to cartridge, you will also vary the performance from cartridge to cartridge. While it is recognized that some excessively compressed powder charges do result in superb accuracy, it is my opinion such loads are the exception and not the rule.

No one can argue the fact that once you start crushing the powder charge, fracturing kernels of powder so they are no longer of their original size and are no longer glazed on all surfaces, then you no longer have the powder charge you started with. You have something different, a mixture of various granulations mingled with powder dust that top shooters would normally separate from the charge by screening. You have a powder charge over which the only control you have is a matter of total weight, for there is no way you can accurately control the weights of the various components of a mixed powder charge acquired by crushing the powder. If you desire a duplex load made up of various granulations of black powder, weigh these various granulations separately. And if your cartridge case will not accommodate a sufficient amount of powder to get the job done, then throat the barrel and go to a tapered bullet or have the chamber recut to accommodate a longer cartridge case.

Whatever your choice, when it comes to powder compression, use some common sense. Although it may be true that the powder charge in our .45-70 government cartridges and most commercially loaded black powder cartridges were compressed to a solid plug of various granulations, these cartridges were not intended for competitive purposes but for military and hunting purposes where targets were usually larger and closer than the metallic silhouettes, and the number of shots permitted was not limited to one per target.

It might also be well to consider that the old-time competitive shooter often breech-loaded his bullet ahead of a cartridge case that was loaded on the firing line with an *uncompressed* charge of powder. That these old-time riflemen shot excellent scores with rifles loaded as described is a matter of record.

9

Neck Tension – How Little?

I believe that if you asked a dozen BPCR shooters why they put neck tension on their bullets, the most common answer would be to prevent the bullet from falling out of the cartridge case when a cartridge was lifted from the box. And another common answer would be to prevent a bullet from being left in the chamber when a loaded cartridge had to be extracted.

While both reasons are valid and justifiable, the primary function of neck tension in a black powder cartridge rifle is to retard the departure of the bullet by a number of microseconds to help assure positive and uniform ignition of the powder charge. Without positive and uniform ignition, you will not get the best of accuracy from your rifle.

Does this mean all black powder cartridges loaded for competition must have at least some neck tension on the bullet? Absolutely not. The same microseconds retardation afforded by neck tension is also influenced by bullet weight, the amount of glazing on the powder and/or the hardness of the powder kernels. Heavy bullets for the caliber involved require more time to get in motion, and hard well-glazed powders require more time to ignite than softer, under-glazed powders.

Let me give you an example. When I first started this BPCR silhouette competition, I full-length resized my fired cartridge cases just enough so I would have some neck tension on the bullets (for the first two reasons given) and so the cartridges would chamber without any interference. My load at the time was 67 grains of GOEX FFg powder fired by a Winchester WLRM primer to drive a 540- to 550-grain Postell bullet.

This worked fine and proved to be what I considered an accurate load. But as time went by and I was shooting in more and more matches, it occurred to me that if I could reload my fired cartridge case without any resizing, I would eliminate three different operations in the loading process – resizing, neck expanding and a light taper crimp. Not only would I eliminate those three operations, I would also eliminate a lot of wear and tear on the brass cartridge cases.

Imagine my surprise when I went to the range and discovered the cartridges fired with no neck tension gave better accuracy than those I had been using that had some neck tension! The difference was clearly noticeable on side-by-side targets, and my standard practice from then on was to load with no neck tension.

Then came the time when I decided to switch from GOEX FFg to GOEX Cartridge. The Cartridge powder had a much heavier glaze and felt somewhat harder than the FFg. I also thought it was a bit more uniform in the size of the kernels than the FFg but am not certain of this. What I am certain of is that when I switched to the Cartridge powder, I started to experience about one off-shot out of every five or six shots fired. And it seemed that no subtle change in the powder charge, primer or compression would eliminate that one off-shot. I even acquired some GOEX Cartridge powder made in October 1995, an excellent powder, but still the off-shots persisted.

Finally, using one of the new Lyman .45-caliber neck-sizing dies, I started neck sizing my cartridge cases to provide a bit of neck tension, and the off-shots disappeared like magic. The difference in the ignition characteristics of the softer GOEX FFg with very little glazing and GOEX Cartridge powder having a much heavier glaze was just enough to require the extra neck tension that would provide uniform ignition from cartridge to cartridge.

As far as the loading of black-powder cartridges for competition is concerned, neck tension is nothing more nor less than one more factor affecting accuracy that must be controlled by the shooter. There are no more hard and fast rules relative to neck tension than there are among the type and thickness of wad one should use. You simply have to recognize the fact that neck tension or total lack of neck tension does affect ignition as does the tightness of the wad, the weight of the bullet and the choice of primer. To state that one *must* have neck tension in order to get good accuracy or if one uses no neck tension then one must compress the powder charge to its limit is in error.

One shooter I know has honed out his neck sizing die so he can just seat his lubricated bullet in the mouth of the case with his fingers. While there is virtually no neck tension on his bullets, neither are his bullets so loose in the case that they will fall out if the cartridge is held with the bullet downward.

If we turn back to some shooting history, we find that one of the American shooters, Lieutenant Fulton, participating in the 1874 international rifle match held at Creedmoor used his Remington rolling block as a breechloading muzzleloader.

That is, the bullet was seated from the muzzle. Since the charged cartridge case was chambered separately and the bullet never entered the cartridge case, there was absolutely no neck tension. If ever there was going to be poor and erratic ignition due to lack of resistance (neck tension) and subsequent pressure buildup, this would be the time.

The same thing applies, but even more so, to all those old-timers who breech-seated their bullets and then chambered a cartridge case filled with powder which, according to Ned Roberts and Ken Waters in their book *The Breech-Loading Single Shot Rifle*, was neither weighed nor compressed. In this case, the bullets being breech-seated were fully engraved by the rifling before firing and offered virtually no resistance other than inertia at the time of firing.

Neither neck tension nor lack of neck tension is a requirement for loading an accurate black-powder cartridge. The requirement is, I believe, a uniform and positive ignition of the powder from shot to shot. And whether you use neck tension, heavy bullets for the caliber involved, a duplex powder charge or a combination of all factors involved is up to you.

A few paragraphs back I mentioned that when I changed from 67 grains of GOEX FFg to 70 grains of GOEX Cartridge, I had to use some neck tension on my bullets to eliminate one off-shot out of every five or six shots. At the time I was using a 545-grain Postell bullet of original design having three driving bands seated within the cartridge case.

Since then I switched from my heavy Postell bullet to the lighter tapered Lyman bullet No. 457675 for which I was involved in the design. With this bullet I am able to use 85 grains of Cartridge powder compressed 0.125 inch with the bullet seated only 0.150 inch deep in the mouth of the case. This is sufficient to cover the rear driving band and one grease groove. There is no crimp.

Although the single driving band being pressed into the mouth of the cartridge case does afford some neck tension, the amount of neck tension is minimal. Yet the cartridges loaded in this manner with the new 513-grain tapered bullet give superlative accuracy, better than the original design Postell I have used for so many years.

If we sift through all the evidence and examples related to neck tension that we have read about, witnessed or experienced first-hand, we might be able to isolate certain conditions where it seems that neck tension could easily be omitted.

First, the old-timers showed us that the small-caliber, small-capacity cartridge cases like the .32-40 and .38-55 were naturals when it came to loading without neck tension. Many, if not most, of their competitive matches involving these cartridges were fired with breech-seated bullets, a condition in which there is no neck tension at all. I personally believe the primary reason for this is that the primer flame in these cartridges is much more concentrated than in the larger .45-70 cartridge case or cases based on the .45-70. Being more concentrated, you get more uniform ignition without the necessity of neck tension to retard the departure of the bullet.

Secondly, it is my opinion, and I want to emphasize this is only an opinion, there seems to be a relationship between the size of the powder charge and a requirement for neck tension. When Lt. Fulton loaded his .44-caliber rolling block from the muzzle in the 1874 Creedmoor match, he was using a powder charge in the range of 90 to 100 grains and possibly more. In my own .45-70, when I went to a lighter bullet but increased the powder charge from 70 to 85 grains and all but eliminated neck tension, the load responded with good accuracy and none of the off-shots that plagued me earlier. And finally, for years I have watched Ron Snover seat his bullets with his fingers just prior to a match. These were all .40-caliber cartridges loaded with 70 to 90 grains of powder. As for accuracy, Ron is one of the very few shooters who has taken 30 consecutive targets over the cross-sticks at Ridgway, Pennsylvania, in a 40-round match.

In each of these three examples, the powder charge used is in the upper range for the caliber or diameter of the bullet involved. It would appear because of this there might be a heat and pressure buildup during the first microseconds of ignition that provides an almost instant and uniform ignition of the entire powder column. Whether or not this is or will be a proven fact, I cannot say. It is merely my opinion.

With everything said and done, do we want to load our black-powder cartridges with neck tension or without neck tension?

While the general answer to that is to do whatever works for you, there are certain advantages to loading without any neck tension. First, if you have a fairly snug chamber in your rifle, then you can often fireform cartridge cases once and never have to touch them again except possibly to trim them. Even this will be an isolated occasion.

If your chamber is large enough to require some neck sizing, then get a neck-sizing die and hone it out just so you can seat the bullets with your fingers. Once this is done, then neck sizing is the only extra operation you have to do during the loading operation. Further, with the amount of neck tension held to a minimum, there is very little working of the brass.

Finally, it is much easier to control *no* neck tension than it is to control *how much* neck tension. Once you decide to use neck tension on bullets being loaded for competitive shooting, then you have to be aware that the amount of neck tension can vary from cartridge to cartridge depending upon the thickness and temper of the brass at the mouth of the case, the inside cleanliness of the mouth of the case, the difference in length of each cartridge case and the variation in the amount of lubricant on the surface of the driving bands of the bullet being seated.

While all these factors may be minor to the point of being virtually unnoticeable as far as accuracy is concerned, they are there and once in awhile could accumulate in combination to the degree that the individual shot you depended upon for the winning score or your own personal record went astray.

10

Should You Season the Barrel?

Before plunging feet first into the subject of barrel seasoning, you should be aware of the fact this section will probably ask more questions than it answers. Furthermore, there will be no recommendations as to how and with what you should season your rifle barrel, or even if you should season it. That is all left for you to decide. I say this because of the many different factors involved, and the fact that one could possibly ruin a good barrel if he or she failed to use good reasoning in the process. More importantly, so little has been said or written on the subject that, as far as I am concerned, most of us who are even thinking about such a thing are in uncharted waters as far as the black powder cartridge rifle is concerned.

With that said, let's take a look at past experiences. I first started using cast bullets in a .30-06 back in 1949, followed a year later with the .45-70 and three years after that with the .375 H&H. In those early years, commercially manufactured metal jacketed bullets were counted and recounted and looked upon with the same affection as one's savings account. And in order to satisfy a voracious appetite for shooting, I had to go to cast bullets, almost always propelled by smokeless powder.

The very first thing I learned in this cast bullet shooting was that one *never* fired metal jacketed bullets prior to and during the same shooting session with cast bullets. Once a handful of jacketed bullets was fired down bore, accuracy with cast bullets deteriorated until the metal fouling from the jacketed bullets was scrubbed out of the barrel.

The next thing I learned – though it was years later while I was using the Ruger Nos. 1 and 3 .45-70s – was that one got better performance from cast bullets if he did not use a powerful metal-removing solvent in the barrel following a shooting session with cast bullets. In short, once the barrel was impregnated with bullet lubricant, it was best to leave it that way as far as cast bullets were concerned. The barrel cleaning process when using cast bullets amounted to nothing more nor less than a few oiled patches through the bore until the next shooting session. If there was any leading present, it was removed with a bronze wire brush.

During this same time frame, there were reports and articles from .22 competitive shooters to the effect that they did not subject their barrels to solvents either, because once you cleaned a .22 barrel with solvents, it took another 100 or 200 rounds to get it properly seasoned again and to restore accuracy to what it had been before the solvent.

Now this was with smokeless powder where one or two or three lightly oiled patches through the bore would remove the powder residue and protect the bore against rust until the next shooting session. Thus it was that shooters using lead alloy bullets recognized the accuracy advantage of a seasoned barrel, a barrel usually seasoned with nothing more nor less than bullet lubricant from the bullets fired down bore.

The black powder cartridge rifle cast bullet shooter is faced with a different set of circumstances than the smokeless powder cast bullet shooter. First and foremost is the black-powder residue or fouling left in the barrel following each shot. If any of this fouling is left in the barrel under a flake of leading or under that which might have been used as barrel dressing or seasoning, you have the potential for rust and a pit in the barrel at that location within a short time.

Faced with this, it behooves the BPCR shooter to use not one but two solvents during the barrel cleaning process. The first solvent is usually a water-based solvent to soften and remove the black-powder fouling, while the second is usually one of the more powerful commercially available solvents used to loosen lead or metal deposits in the barrel. Following this cleaning procedure with the solvents, the bore is usually dried and then protected from rust with a lightly oiled patch or, as some shooters prefer, a clean patch saturated with a solvent like Hoppe's No. 9, which will continue to work on or loosen any flake of lead left in the bore. Thus, it is almost always a foregone conclusion that a petroleum-based product is left in the barrel to protect the bore.

While I cannot say with absolute certainty that all petroleum-based products have a tendency to harden black-powder fouling, I do know at least some of them have this characteristic. I have tried them in various bullet lubes and found them wanting. Even if a dry patch is pushed through the bore just prior to the next shooting session, there still may be some petroleum residue left in the bore that will have a tendency to harden the black-powder fouling. Hardened black-powder fouling is the bane of all black powder cartridge rifle shooters. It is a cause of many a drastic shift in point of impact as well as the occasional off-shot, particularly on days of low humidity. And it is totally unpredictable.

With this in mind, it seems to me that the black powder cartridge rifle shooter has three options when it comes to maintaining the rifle barrel. The first option is to continue to do what most of us have been doing for the past several years. That is, forget about barrel seasoning and remove the black-powder fouling with a solvent made expressly for that purpose. Follow this with one of the powerful solvents made for loosening and removing metal fouling, and finally leave the bore protected with a light film of oil or one of the solvents recommended for that purpose. Before the next shooting session, run two or three clean, dry patches through the bore so you have a clean, dry bore for the first shot.

The second option is to remove the black-powder fouling and metal fouling as in the first option. Then, after running several dry patches through the bore, saturate a patch with your chosen bore dressing and work it back and forth in the bore several times to make certain the bore is thoroughly coated with a thin film of the dressing. Leave this dressing in the bore during your next shooting session.

Warning: When applying a bore dressing, always make certain to use a chamber guide on the cleaning rod to prevent leaving any bore dressing in the chamber. Following application of the bore dressing, thoroughly clean the chamber with two or three dry patches. Leaving bore dressing in the chamber greatly increases back thrust on the

breechblock and could result in serious injury or possible death.

The third option is to remove the black-powder fouling with a solvent made expressly for that purpose. Thoroughly wire brush the bore, followed by two or three clean, dry patches to remove any deposits of lead fouling, and then dress the bore as explained in option two. The object in this option is to *never* use a metal fouling solvent in the bore (as this will also remove any previous seasoning) but to thoroughly season the bore by impregnating the pores in the metal with a suitable dressing and then always keeping it in a seasoned condition. The critical point with this option is to make certain there is no minute deposit of powder fouling or metal fouling trapped underneath the dressing.

When it comes to the barrel dressing itself, we have a number of choices to consider. First we have Lyman's Super Moly Bore Cream, a moly-based dressing developed especially for treating rifle bores. It is easy to apply, and just a little bit of it goes a long way.

Another bore dressing, which is extremely popular among the muzzleloaders, is the Thompson/Center 1000 Plus Bore Butter. I am told that among the muzzle-loading community, this is widely used by those shooting Maxi-Balls, a situation not too far removed from that of our black powder cartridge rifles. T/C's 1000 Plus is available in 5-ounce tubes and is labeled as "An all purpose firearm protectant that inhibits rust," and "An all-natural gun care product that seasons the bore – in black powder rifles."

While I have never tried the next product as a barrel dressing, one top-notch barrel maker has been quoted as saying: "Go to Walmart and find the Slick 50 shelf and get a quart off the back row and do not shake the container; keep (it) in an upright position. After checking out of the store, go to your vehicle, remove the oil cap on your motor and very easily pour off the top $\%_0$ of the 'goo'! On the bottom will be what you want; a white filmy looking 'goo' that you pour off into a small container to keep in your gun box. Wet a patch with the 'goo' and wipe through the bore after a few shooting sessions and see what develops."

I have further read that Slick 50 is made of 30wt castor oil and Teflon, and if this is true, it would ease any concerns about using a petroleum derivative in a black powder cartridge rifle. However, I would like to point out that castor oil is also used in making soap because it is a humectant (promotes retention of moisture). Although I have used castor oil in bullet lubricants to good success, and know of others who are doing the same, I hesitated in trying it as a bore dressing because of this characteristic. Instead, I took a block of mild steel about one inch wide by four inches long, finished one side off to a high polish and then swabbed the surface with castor oil. Since the castor oil was thicker than it would be in a rifle barrel, I then laid a paper towel on it to absorb the excess. This done, a large drop of water was placed on the surface of the steel.

Within three hours the drop of water had turned a rusty brown, and by next morning the water had evaporated leaving a small deposit of rust that was easily wiped off with a paper towel.

Later I tried the same test on the same block of steel with pure neat's-foot oil. The first drop of water evaporated within three hours leaving the surface of the steel bright and shiny. Thinking there had been too little water for a good test, a four or five-drop puddle of water was left on the steel overnight and by morning had evaporated leaving the steel as bright and shiny as before.

Now this in no way can be considered conclusive. It cannot even be considered a close cousin to a laboratory test. And while I know castor oil has been used as a lubricant in early aircraft engines and many other lubricating applications, I also know from personal experience that pure neat's-foot oil makes one of the best patch lubricants I ever used in a flintlock. Many times I have left a patched ball in my Great Plains flintlock for three weeks and even longer, and when the ball was pulled, the patch was still moist with neat's-foot oil with absolutely no hint or indication of rust. I have also used pure neat's-foot oil in black powder bullet lubes with good success.

If you feel the urge to try pure neat's-foot oil, make certain it is labeled 100 percent pure neat's-foot oil. Do not attempt to use that which is labeled Neatsfoot Compound. Further, neat's-foot oil contains small solid particles that should be removed prior to using neat's-foot oil as a barrel dressing. To do this, strain the oil through six layers of clean cheese cloth three successive times. Use clean cheese cloth each time.

Now that we have discussed barrel dressings and the options for applying barrel dressings, why in the world would anyone want to go to all the fuss and bother? Why not clean and protect the barrel as outlined in the first option and be done with it? By doing that, one can be certain of having a clean, well-protected barrel with all the metal fouling and black-powder fouling removed.

One of the primary answers is that when I get on the

firing line for a run at the silhouettes, I do not want to waste my first sighter shot. If my first sighter shot is on the target, I want to *know* that my second shot is going to be in the same group. If my first sighter shot is off the target, I want to *know* I can make a precise sight adjustment and be confident of a hit on the target with the second shot. Dressing the bore of your rifle as described in the second and third options almost always gives you the advantage of having the first shot inside the natural group. Shooters who go to the line with a clean, dry bore seldom have this advantage.

Second, if you are going to put leading in the barrel, it usually starts with the first shot from a clean, dry bore. And once you have leading, regardless of how little, successive shots often build upon it and accuracy deteriorates. Shooting that first shot through a well-dressed barrel goes a long way toward preventing any leading at all.

Third, as I said at the beginning of this discussion, I noticed years ago when shooting cast bullets from my .375 H&H and .45-70 Rugers that the rifles shot much better with greater consistency if I did not use a metal removing solvent in the bores. Once the bore was seasoned with cast bullet lubricant, I never subjected it to a strong solvent until I was ready to switch to metal jacketed bullets.

So how do I treat the bore of my .45-70 silhouette rifle today? For many years at the end of each match, I did what most shooters do. That is, as described in the first option, I removed the black-powder fouling with a solvent made for that purpose. Following that, the barrel was dried and then all metal fouling was removed with Ed's Red bore solvent and snug fitting patches and bronze wire brushes. Finally, the bore was dried and then protected with two or three lightly oiled patches or patches wet with Break Free.

From that procedure, I moved into the second option where I clean the barrel with black powder fouling solvent followed with the Ed's Red solvent. Then the barrel is dried, followed with a patch saturated with clear, pure neat's-foot oil. The neat's-foot oil is left in the bore for the first shot at the next shooting session.

At the present time, as I sit writing this, I have replaced my usual black-powder solvent and Ed's Red solvent with Butch's Black Powder Bore Shine marketed by Lyman Products, Inc. According to its 2002 catalog, this new solvent is odorless, non-toxic, non-flammable, biodegradable and protects against rust and corrosion. It comes from a special cleaning solvent used by the U.S. military and is claimed to remove powder, lead and plastic fouling faster than any other cleaner. After cleaning the barrel with Butch's Black Powder Bore Shine, the bore is thoroughly dried and then dressed with pure neat's-foot oil, which is left in the bore for the next shooting session.

Although this new solvent seems quite mild when compared to Ed's Red and some of the other commercial metal removing solvents on the market, I believe it also removes any previous dressing left in the barrel. And while I believe it would be preferable not to remove previous dressing but to let it impregnate the minute pores in the metal, I also believe that at this stage of the game this procedure is about the best we can do.

Sometime in the future, I would like to move into the third option where I simply clean the bore of all black-powder fouling with nothing more than a water-based solvent, and then dress it with pure neat's-foot oil.

Is this so much different from what many of the old-time hunters did? Didn't most of these grizzled, old shooters treat the bore of their rifles with sperm oil? Or bear oil? Did any of them ever write about using any solvent stronger than boiling water for cleaning the bore of their rifle?

You figure it out, and then treat your barrel accordingly. As I said in the beginning, I am not going to make any recommendation one way or the other, because this is a situation where the lack of common sense and good judgment could ruin a good barrel. It is also a situation where the employment of common sense and good judgment might help the performance of your barrel.

11

Make Your Own Bullet Lubricant

Bullet lubricants for the black powder cartridge rifle come in many different textures, colors, odors and combinations of animal and vegetable waxes, oils and fats. Some work exceptionally well in most rifles, some in a few rifles and none in all rifles under all conditions. To make a serious claim that one particular bullet lubricant is superior to all others is an exercise in showmanship or Madison Avenue advertising. It just isn't so. The bullet lubricant that exhibits *all* the top-quality characteristics desirable for the black powder cartridge rifle has yet to be developed. All too often, in fact almost every time in the development of a bullet lubricant, a tradeoff of one desirable characteristic is made in favor of another. Whether you recognize it at the time or not, that is the nature of the beast.

If you are serious about making up or developing a good bullet lubricant for yourself and/or for some shooting cronies, you must start by using the proper tools for accurate measurement and by recording exactly what you have done. This means you get a good quality digital food scale that will weigh all your substances to ⅛ ounce. If you go into saponified lubricants, which we will discuss later, you will need a good electronic powder scale for weighing precise amounts of sodium hydroxide – lye. You might also do yourself a favor in the domestic department by purchasing your own mixing kettles, starting off with a good double boiler or two different sized kettles that will serve the same purpose.

Again, if you even think about saponified lubricants, your mixing containers should be of stainless steel or the enameled variety. Lye will react with aluminum. You will need one or two sturdy plastic or stainless steel, long-handled stirring spoons for mixing your oils and waxes. And finally, you will want some one-pint plastic all-purpose food storage containers, available from most supermarkets. These are for bulk lube containers. Later we will tell how to make a mould for casting the lubricant in hollow stick form.

When purchasing the kettles, give some thought as to how much lubricant you plan to mix at one time. This is important as some of the lubricants – especially those that are saponified – have a strong tendency toward violent reaction when a particular soap or lye solution is added. Always purchase a kettle that has two or three times the capacity of the amount of lubricant you plan to make. That is, if you plan on mixing two pounds (one quart) at a time, purchase a three-quart mixing kettle.

Before we get into the lube making itself, you should exercise some caution as to what you put into your lubricant. Don't haul off and add some exotic commercial substance without doing a bit of research on its components. Years ago when I was young and brash and full of vinegar, I purchased a one-pound can of "scientifically manufactured" water pump grease from a nearby auto supply store. Now this grease was intended for lubricating the water pump on some of the old cars that graced our highways at the time, and for that purpose it was probably good. It was also just the right consistency for bullet lubricant on the large, heavy bullets I was shooting in the .45-70 and a .54-caliber New Model 1863 Sharps at that time.

The Sharps belonged to a neighbor whose grandfather had carried it home from the Civil War. It was in beautiful condition with an absolutely perfect bore, and for a bullet, I purchased the Lyman mould 533476 Minié ball designed for .54-caliber muskets and some .52 calibers.

In shooting the Sharps rifle, I soon discovered that after one or two shots the fouling from the black powder paper cartridges would bind up the breechblock to the extent it was very difficult to open. I also found out that by putting a generous gob of this "scientifically manufactured" water pump grease on the lip of the chamber before firing greatly alleviated the condition, and I proceeded to fire dozens of rounds through the old rifle in this manner.

After every shooting session the Sharps was thoroughly cleaned with boiling water poured through the bore and then thoroughly dried and oiled. When I returned the rifle, it was in just as good condition as when I borrowed it. A few months later the bore of the barrel was rusted beyond all recognition.

At that time I did not realize what the culprit was and went ahead and mixed some of this water pump grease into some bullet lubricant being used on cast bullets for my Winchester Model 70 .375 H&H. These were fired with smokeless powder and, again after each shooting session, the rifle was thoroughly cleaned and oiled.

However, within two days after each cleaning, the barrel was rusted on the inside, and it didn't matter what I used to remove the rust and clean the bore, the rust would return within a day or so.

To shorten the story, there was something in the water pump grease that permeated the pores in the metal of rifle barrels and created rust in quantity. I managed to save the barrel on the Winchester, but the old Sharps barrel was ruined forever. Before adding any exotic materials to your bullet lubricant, do a bit of research to learn exactly what you are adding.

If you are like most BPCR shooters, the climax to the whole operation of making a bullet lubricant is to load up a handful of cartridges and go to the range. While there is nothing wrong with this, the only way to perform a reliable test on bullet lubricant is to use a load and bullet that is known to give good accuracy in the rifle in which the lubricant is to be tested. That is, use the very best, most accurate load and bullet combination you have and do not change *anything* except the bullet lubricant.

You will also do well to make a note of the temperature and humidity at the range during the time of firing. This might mean you will have to purchase a $10 combination thermometer/hygrometer at the local hardware, but it will also tell you the reason you got such poor accuracy with your new lubricant was not because of the lubricant, but because you did not put enough air through the blow tube to soften the fouling! Those who put a damp patch through the barrel after each shot are seldom faced with this problem, but since most shooters today use the blow tube to soften fouling, humidity and temperature merit considerable attention when testing a bullet lubricant.

Precise accuracy is always the primary objective when developing a bullet lubricant for the black powder cartridge rifle. Without accuracy, nothing else counts. And believe me, there is a difference in accuracy in different rifles with different bullet lubricants. In the first chapter of my book *How-To's for the Black Powder Cartridge Rifle Shooter* on pages 2 and 8 are recipes for two different bullet lubricants. The first recipe uses a mixture of beeswax, pure neat's-foot oil and Murphy's Oil Soap™, while in the second recipe the Murphy's Oil Soap is replaced with Neutrogena® Facial Soap (original formula). Both lubricants work good in the black powder cartridge rifle. In fact, I used the first lubricant containing the Murphy's Oil Soap for many years including July 26, 1998, when I made a successful long run of 59 pigs.

While the second lubricant using the Neutrogena Facial Soap never gave me quite the precise accuracy as the first, Dr. Peter L. Fry of Australia found that the second lubricant when used in his rifle provided the superlative accuracy needed for silhouette and long-range shooting. Even more recently I developed another lubricant that gave leading in my rifle while eliminating leading problems for other shooters!

Bullet lubricants for the black powder cartridge rifle are as fickle as the primers used for the same rifle. What works well for one shooter may be a disaster for the next. There is no best bullet lubricant and there are none that will give you all the desirable characteristics in all rifles under all conditions. Perhaps someday, but not today.

There are two basic types of BPCR bullet lubricants, the non-saponified and the saponified. Each of them has its advantages and disadvantages. The non-saponified is by far the most common type, and is simply a mixture of oils, waxes and fats in such combination as to meet the needs of the shooter. The non-saponified bullet lubricant usually has a low melting point, often around 120 to 125 degrees, which makes it suitable for pan lubing, but vulnerable to hot barrels during the summer heat. Under these conditions it is not uncommon for the lubricant to melt off the bullet in the chamber of the rifle, causing all sorts of problems from leading to hardened black-powder fouling.

The saponified bullet lubricant differs from the non-saponified in that after the melting and final mixing of the components, a lye solution is added. This causes a chemical reaction (which can be violent) that hardens the lubricant and raises the melting point a significant amount. Of much greater importance to the BPCR shooter, a saponified bullet lubricant is water soluble to some extent. That is, any residual lubricant left in the bore along with the powder fouling readily mixes with water or moisture from the blow tube when you blow three or four deep breaths through the barrel following each shot. This, I believe, helps soften the fouling to a greater extent than with a non-saponified lubricant.

The downside of the saponified bullet lubricant is that it is more complex to make and often cannot be remelted for pan lubing. It also often gels up so rapidly after stirring in the lye solution that you cannot pour it into a hollow stick mould but have to put it in one-pint plastic food containers to harden. If you are using a Redding-SAECO lubri-sizer, this is no problem, but for those lubri-sizers having a center screw in the reservoir, it is a bit more difficult to recharge the lubri-sizer with bullet lubricant unless it is in the hollow stick form.

A few paragraphs back I made reference to two bullet

lubricants developed in 1993 and mentioned in my book *How-To's for the Black Powder Cartridge Rifle Shooter*. The recipe for the first lube that I called No. 1 is as follows:

Matthews No. 1

Yellow beeswax . . . . .2 parts (ounces avoirdupois)

Pure neat's-foot oil . . .1 part (fluid ounces)

Murphy's Oil Soap . . . .1 part (fluid ounces)

This is an excellent bullet lubricant, and although it is not saponified, the Murphy's Oil Soap raises the melting point to 146 degrees, the same as beeswax. In making this lubricant, melt the beeswax first in a double boiler and then add the neat's-foot oil, stirring it into the beeswax until it is thoroughly mixed. Unless the neat's-foot oil was prewarmed by standing the container in a kettle of hot water while the beeswax was melting, it will probably congeal to a certain extent as it is added to the beeswax. If this happens, just keep on stirring until it heats up and thoroughly mixes with the beeswax.

After the neat's-foot oil and beeswax are thoroughly mixed and there is no indication of congealing in the mixture, then you can *slowly* add the Murphy's Oil Soap. Do this very slowly to start with. Sometimes, especially if you are making up a large batch of lubricant, there is a violent reaction when the Murphy's Oil Soap is first added. For a few seconds the mixture will boil up in the kettle, and it is at this time that you must stir it vigorously and be grateful you purchased a large capacity mixing kettle.

After the boiling subsides, you can usually add the rest of the Murphy's Oil Soap, stirring continuously until you have a nice solid-color, creamy mixture. The lubricant can then be poured into hollow-stick moulds or into the plastic food containers.

If you want a bullet lubricant containing molybdenum disulphide, add one ounce of moly per pound of bullet lubricant (5.88 percent) after the Murphy's Oil Soap has been thoroughly mixed in. For this purpose, I have always used and recommend the Superfine Grade Moly Powder sold by Lyman. This stuff is really fine, and a little of it goes a long way. You do not need any more than the one ounce of moly for every pound of bullet lubricant.

Warning: When measuring or pouring molybdenum disulphide, wear a dust mask to prevent inhalation of any of this substance. Also avoid getting it into your eyes. Read the safety instructions printed on the package.

Early in 1995 a modified form of the No. 1 lubricant was developed. This was called the No. 2.

Matthews No. 2

Yellow beeswax	.8 ounces
Pure neat's-foot oil	.4 fluid ounces
Neutrogena® Facial Soap (original formula)	.1 cake (3.5 ounces)

Again, melt the beeswax in a double boiler and then stir in the neat's-foot oil. As soon as they are thoroughly mixed with no further congealment, slice the soap into long peels and add it to the mixture. This soap will quickly melt, but do not let the mixture get too hot or it will start to boil.

This, too, is a good non-saponified bullet lubricant, though I never did get quite the accuracy from it that I obtained from the No. 1. Whether that was due to some quirk of my rifle or pure happenstance during the few times I tested it, I don't know. As mentioned earlier, Dr. Peter Fry of Australia is a superb rifleman and competitor, and he uses the No. 2 almost to the exclusion of everything else.

Now, a word about the addition of soap to a bullet lubricant. First, I want it understood that my knowledge of chemistry is limited to about eight weeks of high school during which time I learned absolutely nothing and remembered all of it! However, from what I have read and what I have seen, many Schuetzen shooters, like many BPCR shooters, make their own bullet lubricant. And in the process often add grated Ivory bar soap or Kirk's Castile soap to the mixture of waxes and oils in order to raise the melting point and to toughen the lubricant. The addition of soap also helps give the lubricant a fine, soapy texture.

The problem in adding these soaps is that because of their high melting temperatures, they have to be melted separately and then quickly added to the lubricant after the lubricant has been brought up to nearly the same temperature as the soap to facilitate the mixing of the two. Heating the waxes and oils to the point where they start to smoke indicates some degree of degradation and, in my opinion, is an operation best left undone.

I strongly suggest that if you want to add soap to your bullet lube, use a liquid like Murphy's Oil Soap, which is labeled as a "pure vegetable oil soap," or partially saponify your bullet lubricant thus making it into a soap. This will be discussed later. As for the Neutrogena Facial Soap, it has a low melting temperature and easily mixes with beeswax and neat's-foot oil. However, I have absolutely no idea what is in Neutrogena Facial Soap.

One of the best non-saponified bullet lubricants I have used in my .45-70 black powder cartridge rifle is:

Matthews Yellow Jacket

Yellow beeswax . . . . .1 part by weight

Thompson/Center 1000 Plus
    Bore Butter . . . . . . .2 parts by weight

This Bore Butter comes in a 5-ounce tube. The easiest way I have found to get it out of the tube is to cut the top of the tube off with a utility knife. Squeeze out all the Bore Butter you can and then cut off the bottom of the tube. Using an old table knife, scrape out the inside of the tube and the top of the tube that you previously cut off. Melt in a double boiler with 2½ ounces of yellow beeswax and then pour off into a hollow-stick mould or into one-pint plastic food containers.

After this lubricant hardens, it seems to be quite brittle, but after putting it under pressure in a lubri-sizer, it becomes soft and flows easily through the ports in the sizing die. It is an excellent lubricant as far as accuracy and leading are concerned but does not seem to contribute as much as I would like toward softening black-powder fouling under low-humidity conditions, that is when the humidity stands at 40 percent or less.

Another non-saponified bullet lubricant that Ron Snover has sometimes used with good success is nothing more nor less than the old NRA mixture of 50 percent Alox 2138F and 50 percent yellow beeswax. This, of course, is available in hollow-stick form and under various names from Lyman as well as other sources. Thinking the addition of 1000 Plus Bore Butter would make the lubricant even better, I mixed up several ounces consisting of:

Alox 2138F	1 part by weight
Yellow beeswax	1 part by weight
1000 Plus Bore Butter	1 part by weight

This gave a lubricant that seemed just about perfect in texture, and I was so pleased with its appearance and feel that I sent a sample to Ron for him to try. Both of us gave this lubricant a number of test firings under different conditions, and both of us came to the same conclusion – forget about it! It just would not give any kind of favorable accuracy.

In the development of bullet lubricants, I found this to be true on many occasions. A mixture that had every reason in the world to give superb performance often failed miserably. Why this should be true, I can only offer an opinion, i.e., some component or combination of components contributes to the hardening of the black-powder fouling instead of softening it. And once you get hard, baked-on fouling in the bore, you will experience abrupt and drastic shifts in point of impact. Sometimes you can make a sight adjustment and the following two or three or four shots will go into the same group area until a change in the fouling takes place causing a subsequent shift in point of impact. At other times you just cannot put two successive shots in the same group area.

One final non-saponified recipe for which I am indebted to Kevin Lewsey, a top silhouette shooter at Wilton, New York, is a simple mixture of 60 percent yellow beeswax and 40 percent castor oil. There are a number of shooters other than Kevin who also use this lubricant at the Wilton matches, and from my observation of the resulting scores, it has to be a superb lubricant.

While I cannot say that the saponified bullet lubricants are superior to the non-saponified, they do have their advantages. First, they are more flexible in the preparation. That is, you can put more oil per unit of beeswax in a saponified lubricant and still control the degree of hardness or softness by the amount of lye that is added during the saponification process. And second, the melting point of a saponified lubricant is always higher than the non-saponified, a very desirable characteristic when shooting under a hot sun. A third advantage, and equally as important as the second, is the fact the saponification process converts or partially converts the lubricant into a soap, and as such, it is to some degree water soluble. As mentioned before, I believe this helps promote softening the powder fouling when a blow tube is used between shots.

In November 2000, after numerous attempts at developing the perfect lubricant based on Oatey's Pipe Lubricant (a potassium soap of vegetable oil) and beeswax, I changed my strategy and developed a saponified bullet lubricant.

Orange Extra No. 6

Yellow beeswax . . . . .1 part by weight

Pure neat's-foot oil . . . . . .1 part by weight

Sodium hydroxide (lye) . . .weight of oil in ounces x 0.129 x 437.5 = weight of lye in grains

Distilled water . . . . .weight of oil in ounces x 0.3 (or 0.33) = weight of water in ounces

A word of explanation relative to the amount of lye and water is needed here. The factor of 0.129 used in the calculation of the amount of lye is a factor developed by custom soap makers to determine how much lye should be used to saponify a given amount of neat's-foot oil to produce a mild soap. This factor will vary with the type of oil or fat used, and it can also be slightly varied to regulate the hardness of the soap or, in this case, the hardness of the lubricant.

Although the amount of distilled water required to make up the lye solution is not that critical, I personally try to use as little as needed, because once the lubricant is applied to the bullet, the water in the lube quickly evaporates and the lube will shrink to a slight degree. I like to keep this shrinkage as slight as possible. I should also mention the lubricant is firmly attached to the bullet and does not separate and fall off. Because the amount of water is not that critical, I usually calculate the amount needed based on each factor (0.3 or 0.33) and then round off one result or the other to the nearest ⅛ ounce.

To make this No. 6 lubricant, use an enameled or stainless steel double boiler. Keep the water in the boiler at a low boil throughout the whole process. While the beeswax is melting, stand the container of neat's-foot oil in a kettle of hot water to warm it through. Just get it warm, not hot. This will keep it from congealing when added to the beeswax. After the beeswax is melted, stir in the neat's-foot oil.

Take the lye and distilled water outside or at the sink in front of an open window and mix it. **Warning: Be certain to use distilled water. Do not preheat the water and do not breathe the fumes while mixing.** Stir continuously until the lye is completely dissolved.

Pour the lye solution into the mixture of beeswax and

neat's-foot oil, and stir the mixture vigorously until it is thoroughly mixed. After the first minute or so of stirring, the lye will start reacting with the oil, and the mixture will usually boil up and foam quite violently. **Stir vigorously!** Gradually the foaming will subside, and the mixture will start to gel or thicken. That is the time to get it out of the kettle into the plastic food containers as it will thicken very rapidly.

This boiling and foaming process is usually dependent upon the amount of lubricant being made. If you are making a trial run of only six or eight ounces, the foaming is usually negligible, but if you are making up two pounds of lubricant, then you had better be using a three-quart kettle in order to contain it all at the height of the foaming process.

When making up a significant amount of lubricant, I always keep stirring the mixture in the double boiler until it does boil and foam, thus indicating the saponification process is taking place. Once or twice during my earlier attempts, I started to pour the lubricant into containers before the boiling and foaming process had taken place. After I had poured it off, then it started the foaming process, and I had a mess on my hands.

The temperature of the mixture also has a lot to do with the violence of the boiling and foaming. Those who make soap by saponifying oils and fats do so at much lower temperatures – 100 to 115 degrees – and the saponification process usually takes several hours. Since the lubricant mixtures are much hotter in order to keep the beeswax in a melted state, the saponification process is much faster and much more violent.

Orange Extra No. 6 is an excellent bullet lubricant

with a melting point of about 160 degrees. I first used it in a match at Wilton on December 10, 2000. My records show the temperatures that day ran between 6 degrees Fahrenheit at the beginning of the match to 36 degrees F. after the match was finished. I used a blow tube and did not clean the rifle between relays. I shot a score of 31 at the age of 75 using my O.T.A. Hepburn built by Ron Snover.

A second saponified lubricant was one incorporating castor oil, a component I believe is an asset to any black powder cartridge rifle bullet lubricant by virtue of the fact it is a humectant – retains moisture. This should enhance a saponified lubricant by retaining more moisture from the blow tube and thus keeping the powder fouling softer.

Orange Extra No. 12

Yellow beeswax . . . . .1 part by weight

Castor oil . . . . .1 part by weight

Pure neat's-foot oil . . .1 part by weight

Lye . . . . .weight of *both* oils in ounces x 0.122 x 437.5 = weight of lye in grains

Distilled water . . . . . .weight of *both* oils in ounces x 0.3 (or 0.33) = weight of water in ounces

The instructions for mixing this lubricant are the same as for mixing the Orange Extra No. 6 lubricant. This, too, is an excellent lubricant, though in my rifle the No. 6 gave less leading and was a better performer.

At this point I want to emphasize that I believe sometimes leading is a characteristic of a particular rifle barrel and/or chamber or bullet alloy and not necessarily a default of the lubricant. When the No. 12 was first developed, samples were sent to various top shooters to try out. Within two weeks one shooter came back wanting to know if any more of the No. 12 was available. He had run the gauntlet of bullet lubricants in an unsuccessful attempt to eliminate a severe leading problem. The No. 12 erased the leading like magic.

Also at that time, Ron Snover said he had never used a better lubricant, and other shooters felt the same. Yet in my rifle, leading with the No. 12 was too severe for good accuracy. My first three to five shots were always good, but after that accuracy fell apart. Even the No. 6 lubricant, as well as it had performed on December 10, 2000, at Wilton gave me more leading than I felt was acceptable. I have to believe this was due to some factor other than the bullet lubricant.

The history of the black powder cartridge rifle tells us that beef tallow played a major part in the bullet lubricants used in these rifles. It was easy to come by, easy to mix with beeswax and other waxes and did its job well. Yet today, beef tallow is seldom mentioned as a desirable component of bullet lubricant.

Contrary to what you often read about beef tallow turning rancid, if the tallow is rendered out and properly strained to remove all particles of flesh and tissue, beef tallow will keep in a covered plastic food container for years.

By itself, beef tallow has far too low a melting point and is not tough enough to be a bullet lubricant on grooved bullets. However, when it is partially saponified, it takes on a whole new character that begs for further development as a bullet lubricant. Using beef tallow that had been rendered out in 1989 (12 years prior to this writing), the following lubricant was developed.

Beef tallow	1 part by weight
Molybdenum disulphide ..	weight of tallow in ounces x 0.0588 x 437.5 = weight of moly in grains
Lye	weight of tallow in ounces x 0.053 x 437.5 = weight of lye in grains
Distilled water	weight of tallow in ounces x 0.3 (or 0.33) = weight of water in ounces

Melt the tallow in a double boiler with the water at a soft boil and then add the molybdenum disulphide, stirring it in until it is thoroughly mixed. Mix the lye solution outside or at the sink in front of an open window. When the lye is totally dissolved, add the solution to the tallow-moly mix and stir until it thickens. Then pour it off into a plastic food container.

You will notice the factor for calculating the amount of lye used in this beef tallow lubricant is very low when compared to that of other lubricants. It takes very little lye to harden beef tallow and to significantly raise the melting point. The melting point of this lubricant is about 140 degrees F.

While this lubricant did not give the desired performance, its texture was about perfect, so I wanted to include it here to show what can be done with the process of saponification. It is my firm belief that perhaps with other oils and beeswax a beef tallow lubricant of superior quality can be developed.

As far as the black powder cartridge rifle shooter is concerned, the development of the saponified bullet lubricant is a wide open field. And I believe that when the one best, perfect BPCR lube is developed, it will be of the saponified variety.

What is that one best, perfect bullet lubricant? In my opinion it will be a lubricant that allows the shooter to take his or her place on the firing line and concentrate only on shooting – not on how many times one has to blow through the blow tube nor if the barrel will hold up for the duration of this relay without leading and/or hardened fouling. That will be the ultimate! But right now I will settle for being able to shoot every match with nothing more than a few puffs through the blow tube after each shot – no cleaning between relays. I have been able to do that a few times and came out with a good score, but I want to be able to do that at every match regardless of weather, temperature, humidity and differences in powder.

For those who are interested in further development of a saponified bullet lubricant, following is a list of the most common oils and tallows with their respective saponification factor for determining the amount of lye to be used for a given amount of tallow or oil. This saponification factor is merely a starting point. If you wish to increase or decrease the amount of lye used for controlling the hardness of the lubricant, my suggestion is to add or subtract from the listed factor by increments of 0.003. The addition of more lye will give a harder lubricant while decreasing the amount of lye will give a softer lubricant.

Saponification Factors:

Bear tallow	0.132	Cottonseed oil	0.132
Beef tallow	0.133	Crisco®	0.129
Neat's-foot oil	0.129	Jojoba oil	0.066
Olive oil	0.128	Lanolin	0.070
Olive pomace oil	0.126	Lard	0.131
Canola oil	0.129	Peanut oil	0.129
Castor oil	0.125	Vegetable shortening	0.129
Chicken fat	0.132	Soybean oil	0.128
Cod liver oil	0.126	Deer tallow	0.131
Corn oil	0.129	Mutton tallow	0.131

These three groups were fired consecutively during the course of load development by Ron Snover in April 1996. The rifle was a Remington Hepburn with one of Ron's own barrels chambered for the .40-70SS cartridge. The bullet used was from a SAECO No. 740 mould and weighed 411 grains. Bullet lubricant was the old N.R.A. mixture of 50/50 Alox 2138F and yellow beeswax.

The top group measures 2³⁄₁₆ inches center to center and was fired over 66½ grains of GOEX FFg. The middle group measures 1½ inches center to center and was fired over 67½ grains of GOEX FFg. The bottom group measures 1⁵⁄₁₆ inches center to center and was fired over 68½ grains of GOEX FFg. All groups fired at 100 yards.

Note the lubricant used was an Alox/beeswax mixture and is not usually thought of as a black-powder lubricant.

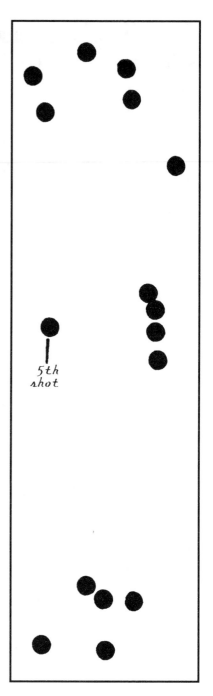

114

12

How to Make a Lube Mould

If you are serious about making you own bullet lubricant, then it follows that you will soon become serious
about casting your lubricant into the 4x1 inch diameter
sticks needed to quickly load the reservoir in your
lubri-sizer. Casting solid sticks for use in the Redding-
SAECO lubri-sizer is much less of a problem than casting hollow sticks for use in the Lyman and RCBS
lubri-sizers, but regardless of which lubri-sizer you use,
casting your lubricant into stick form saves a lot of time
when loading the reservoir of your lubri-sizer.

While there are probably many different ways of making a suitable mould for this purpose, the mould
described here is simple and easy to make, easy to use
and can be used to cast either the solid or hollow lube
sticks.

Bill of Materials:

- 8x8x¼ metal plate (steel, cast iron, aluminum) (1)

- 17 inch long x 1 inch rigid copper tubing (3)

- 1 inch copper tubing end cap (3)

- 18 inch long x ⁵⁄₁₆ inch cold rolled steel rod (3) [for hollow stick mould only]
- No. 10x32 thread x 1 inch long round-head screw (3)
- ¼ inch x 20 thread x 1 inch long cap screw with nut and lock washer (4)

The metal plate can be just about any piece of scrap metal you can locate just so it is about 8 inches square and ¼ inch thick. The plate I used was a cast iron door off an old chimney flue clean-out.

Proceed as follows:

1. Scribe a line across the middle of the plate, and mark the location for three holes along this line. Make the holes 2 inches in from the side of the plate and the third hole in the center of the plate.

2. Using a No. 21 drill, drill the three holes and tap them with a No. 10x32 thread tap.

3. Using a No. 12 drill, drill a hole through the center of each copper end cap.

4. Using a No. 21 drill, drill a hole about 1¼ inches deep in the end of each steel rod. Tap each hole with a No. 10x32 thread tap.

5. Using a No. 7 drill, drill a hole through each corner of the metal plate and tap each hole with a ¼x20 thread.

6. Take one of the ¼-inch cap screws and thread a nut on it about one-third of the way down. Place a lock washer on the nut and thread the cap screw into one of the holes in the corner of the plate. Thread it in until the end of the cap screw is flush with the opposite side of the plate. Secure the cap screw with the nut and lock washer. Do the same with the other

three ¼-inch cap screws. These cap screws serve as legs for the metal plate.

7. If you want to set up for casting the hollow sticks of lubricant, thread the three No. 10 round-head screws up through the bottom side of the plate until they are tight.

8. Set the three end caps over the protruding ends of the No. 10 screws and then thread one of the ⁵⁄₁₆-inch steel rods onto each screw and tighten it against the inside bottom of the end cap.

9. Place one of the lengths of copper tubing down over each steel rod and seat it into the end cap.

10. If you want to set up for casting the solid sticks of lubricant, attach each of the three end caps to the *top* of the plate by threading a No. 10 round-head screw down through the end cap and plate until it is tight. Note: The screws may have to be shortened ¼ inch so the plate will sit level.

11. Place one of the lengths of copper tubing into each end cap.

When actually casting the lubricant into sticks, set the mould in the bottom of the sink. Pour the lube into each copper tubing and then fill the sink with cold water to harden the lube. As the lubricant hardens, you will note it keeps shrinking at the top leaving a deep center cavity. When this happens, fill the tubing again. You may have to do this three or four times during the cooling process.

Let the lubricant thoroughly harden, overnight if practical, before attempting to remove it from the moulds. If you have cast the hollow-stick lube, grasp one of the lengths of copper tubing and rotate it clockwise. This will usually break the tubing loose from the lube and allow you to lift off the tubing. Then try to break the lube free from the steel rod by rotating it clockwise. If this does not work, unscrew the rod and lube from the end cap. Hold it vertically over a work bench with the protruding end of the rod downward and bring it down sharply against the bench until the lube breaks loose from the rod. Once the lube is loosened from the rod, grasp the end of the rod in a vise and pull the lube off.

If you have cast solid sticks of lubricant, simply lift the tubing and lubricant from the end caps and try to jar the lube loose from the tubing with a length of 1-inch wooden dowel. Sometimes it helps to put the tubing and lube in the freezer for a few hours, and sometimes it helps to run hot water over the tubing until the lube can be pushed from the tubing.

Regardless of whether you have cast solid sticks or hollow sticks of bullet lubricant, if you fill all three tubing moulds, you now have three sticks of bullet lubricant, each of them 16 to 17 inches long. Using a sharp, thin-bladed knife, cut each of these sticks into four equal lengths and wrap them separately with waxed paper or food wrapping paper. An even better way is to get a package of Ziploc® snack bags and put two sticks of lubricant into each bag.

Making your own bullet lubricant puts a whole new perspective on black powder cartridge rifle shooting. Although it adds more time to an already time-consuming activity, you truly begin to see the minor differences in bullet lubricants and begin to customize your lubricant for your load and rifle. Casting the lubricant into suitable sticks saves time at the loading bench.

13

Tapered Bullets and Throats

I have always believed the more of the bullet you can put into the barrel before firing, the greater is the potential for superior accuracy. This philosophy has been well substantiated by Schuetzen shooters of the late 1800s as well as those of today who mechanically breech-seat their bullets. And it was substantiated by the Sharps shooters of one and a quarter centuries ago who fired paper patched bullets having a patched diameter so close to bore size they could be seated well within the bore of the rifle. A drawing of an original 550-grain, long-range Sharps paper patched bullet indicates an unpatched diameter of 0.446 inch and a patched diameter of 0.452 inch.

When it comes to the black powder cartridge rifle and competitive shooting at the steel silhouettes, the one-minute allowance for each shot for score does not give time for mechanical breech seating plus blow tubing and making sight adjustments between shots. And while paper patched bullets can give superb accuracy, the wraparound patch is vulnerable to damage when seated in a fouled chamber during a long series of shots.

With the grooved, lubricated bullet and fixed ammunition being by far the most popular among BPCR shooters, many of these shooters have their barrels throated so bullets can be seated well out, thus putting more of the bullet into the barrel before firing and, at the same time, increasing the powder capacity of the cartridge case. In my own .45-70 silhouette rifles, the chambers are throated deeply enough to permit seating bullets out far enough to expose two front driving bands and two grease grooves. This lets me use a powder charge of 67 grains of GOEX FFg or 70 grains of GOEX Cartridge with a 0.060 inch thick wad and from 0.060 to .100 inch compression. Without the throating, my powder charge would be reduced by 5 grains, and the accuracy potential would suffer as well.

Even with the chamber throated as described, bullets having five driving bands are seated 0.400 inch deep in the cartridge case, leaving a lot of room for improvement. But merely extending the throat to accommodate more of the bullet is not necessarily the proper solution, because once you put an exceptionally long throat in a rifle barrel, you are locked into using bullets that will fill that throat. Using bullets whose driving bands do not fill the throat usually results in a reduction of accuracy.

Improvement in my rifles was made possible in the summer of 2000 when Ed Schmitt, manager of product planning at Lyman Products, Inc. asked me to think about a tapered bullet design for the .45-caliber black powder cartridge rifles. Between the two of us we came up with the Lyman 457675 tapered bullet. According to the drawing, the front driving band was to have a diameter of 0.448 inch, the second driving band at 0.449 inch, the third driving band at 0.453 inch and the last three driving bands at 0.459 to 0.460 inch. When cast of a 20-to-1 lead-tin alloy, the bullet weighed about 512 grains.

In my throated barrels, this permitted seating the bullet only 0.150 inch deep in the mouth of the cartridge case, thus putting almost ¾ inch of driving bands into the barrel before firing! It also increased the powder capacity of the .45-70 cartridge case from 70 grains of GOEX Cartridge powder to 85 grains without increasing the amount of powder compression. This is an extremely significant amount and flattened my trajectory by three to five minutes of angle.

Most important was the accuracy. Using this tapered bullet or any similarly tapered bullet in a throated barrel brings you just about as close to a breech-seated bullet as you can get without actually breech-seating it. When a cartridge loaded with this tapered bullet is chambered in a barrel throated to the same depth as Ron Snover throated my barrels, the two front driving bands are within the bore of the barrel, while the third driving band is contacting the rifling about midway within the leade. The next two driving bands are within the 0.459 inch diameter throat with the leading band contacting the root of the rifling.

With a bullet so dimensioned and cast of a 20-to-1 lead-tin alloy, upon the instant of firing and the initial forward movement of the bullet, with the forward section of the bullet bumping up or obturating, you will have four driving bands engaged with the rifling by the time the bullet has moved forward the full width of one driving band! More than that, by using a Pope-style bullet as the basic design, that is a bullet with a short nose and a long body having multiple grooves and driving bands, you virtually assure the axis of the bullet exactly coincides with the axis of the bore.

Consider this for a moment. If we take the cylindrical portion of a cast bullet – even though it may be slightly out of round – and press it into a rifled barrel, that cylindrical section of bullet automatically conforms to the shape of the inside of the rifle barrel, and the axis of that cylindrical section coincides exactly with the axis of the barrel.

However, if you take that same cylindrical section of bullet and add a long Postell-style nose on it and again press it into a rifle barrel, the cylindrical section will again conform to the shape of the inside of the rifle barrel with the axis of the cylindrical section coinciding with the axis of the barrel. But what about the axis of the nose? The nose of the bullet is not reshaped by the inside of the rifle barrel, and the axis of the nose may or may not coincide with that of the cylindrical section of the bullet or with that of the barrel. The difference may be slight, but it may well exist! Thus to me, the moral of the story is that for best accuracy use a bullet having a long cylindrical body with just enough nose on it to provide good aerodynamics. Then add a slight taper to that bullet so most of it is within the rifle barrel before firing.

There is nothing new about tapered bullets. They have been with us for over 100 years. An old Lyman Ideal bullet chart I have shows two tapered bullets apparently designed by or for Dr. Walter G. Hudson, who was a top offhand shooter from about 1898 until well into the twentieth century. One bullet, 319273, is for the .32-40 cartridge and has the three front driving bands at 0.316 inch diameter and the two rear driving bands at 0.323 inch diameter. The other bullet, 375272, is for the .38-55 and weighs 310 grains. While the chart does not show the driving band diameters of this bullet, it is evident from the illustration on the chart that the three front driving bands are smaller in diameter than the two rear bands. Both bullets have a very short nose. While these two Hudson bullets are actually two-diameter bullets rather than tapered, the concept of getting more of the bullet into the barrel before firing is the same.

Among members of the Cast Bullet Association, who take their cast bullet shooting as seriously as anyone, there has been much use made of what is known as an Ardito throat. If memory serves me correctly, I believe this was developed by one John Ardito and is basically a long, tapered throat beginning at the end of the chamber and extending forward at a very slight angle to merge with the rifling. A bullet mould is then cut to produce a tapered bullet whose taper coincides with the taper in the throat. Thus, when only the base band of the bullet is seated in the cartridge case and the cartridge is chambered, almost the entire bullet is within the tapered throat and is aligned with the axis of the bore as nearly as is mechanically possible.

While I have never had any experience with an Ardito throat, the SAAMI chamber specifications for the .458 Winchester Magnum as shown on page 289 of the *NRA Handloading* manual by Wm. C. Davis, Jr., published in January 1981, indicates a tapered throat 1.115 inches long cut at an angle with the axis of the bore of 0 degrees, 29 minutes and 30 seconds. While this may or may not be the same angle as an Ardito throat, it is surely the same concept though perhaps for the purpose of reducing chamber pressure rather than enhancing cast bullet accuracy.

Be that as it may, my Ruger No. 1 chambered for the .458 Winchester cartridge has such a throat and proved to be one of the best smokeless powder cast bullet rifles I ever owned. With the throat merging into the rifling, there is no definitive end of the throat and beginning of the rifling as there is with a straight throat. It is simply a long, smooth transition from throat to rifling that handled the 530-grain RCBS 45-500-FN bullet cast relatively soft at 9 Brinell hardness number (BHN) and fired over 60 grains of H-375 powder for an average velocity of 1,819 fps. An even better load was the same bullet fired over 55 grains of IMR-4064 for an average velocity of 1,659 fps. Even at these velocities, which are well over that of black powder, and with a relatively soft bullet, accuracy was good and there was never a hint of any leading problem.

Although it might seem we have wandered from the basic subject, the point should be well noted that we have barely scratched the surface of tapered bullets and/or tapered throats in the black powder cartridge rifle. I have heard of BPCR shooters who are using tapered bullets, and my friend Jerry Matalavage has recently had Steve Brooks cut a mould based on the original style Postell bullet but with the two front driving bands reduced in diameter so the bullet can be seated well forward in the cartridge case and in the chamber of the rifle.

The tapered bullet opens a whole new perspective for the black powder cartridge rifle shooter. Depending upon whether or not your barrel is throated, the use of a tapered bullet significantly increases the powder capacity of the cartridge case. And by aligning the front of the bullet with the bore of the barrel, and the rear of the bullet with the throat, the potential for better accuracy is greatly improved.

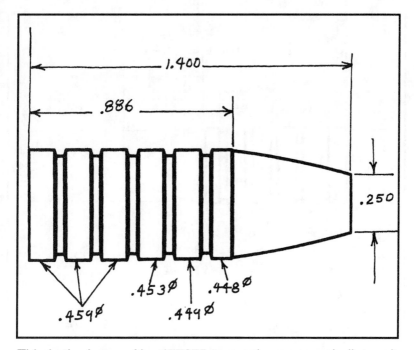

This is the Lyman No. 457675 tapered nose-pour bullet as it was first produced in December 2001. Later moulds for this same bullet had a slightly larger radius on the ogive but with the same diameter meplat and driving bands. The diameters of the first three driving bands were carefully worked out by Ed Schmitt, taking into consideration SAAMI chamber specifications and the prospect of black-powder fouling near the origin of rifling. This bullet has proved superbly accurate.

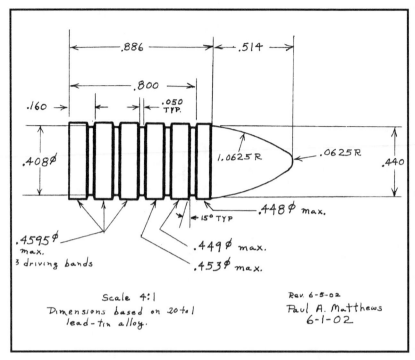

.886

.514

.800

.160

.050 TYP.

.408∅

1.0625 R

.0625 R

.440

.448∅ max.

15° TYP

.4595∅ max.
3 driving bands

.449∅ max.

.453∅ max.

Scale 4:1
Dimensions based on 20 to 1
lead-tin alloy.

Rev. 6-5-02
Paul A. Matthews
6-1-02

This is a revised version of the Lyman tapered bullet 457676. Basically it is identical to the Lyman bullet except for the semi-spitzer nose that makes it less vulnerable to deflection in a 12 o'clock wind. Bullet weight from a 20-to-1 lead-tin alloy averages 500 grains. The first mould cut for this bullet was a base-pour mould made by Steve Brooks in June 2002.

14

Reflections

In looking back over 10 years and 166 competitive BPCR silhouette matches, I have to believe the greatest thing about this game is the people involved in it. During 76 years of life, I have met and been in close contact with thousands of people, but never in all those years did I meet a group of people – an entire community, if you will – who embrace such traditional values as honesty, integrity, loyalty and just plain common decency. Never in these past 10 years with BPCR shooters have I been ashamed of the language used by match participants or been reluctant to have my wife accompany me at a match because of the language used. By their very nature, these people are traditionalists. If that were not true, they would not be shooting black powder.

In a day and age when it is politically incorrect to even speak favorably of rifles or guns in general, does anyone ever really take a close look at competitive shooting and compare our actions as a group with those of other sports? If they did, they would see shoot-off losers shaking hands with winners. They would see the more knowledgeable and more experienced shooters giving advice and exchanging information with those just getting started. And they would see husband and wife, father and son and father and daughter teams on the firing line, a family participation virtually unknown in other sports.

What other competitive sport can you attend and see tens of thousands of dollars worth of equipment standing unattended in racks or in the backs of pick-up trucks and vans? Equipment momentarily left unattended with the knowledge it is safe and secure.

Name one other sport where so much ability and knowledge and skill must come from the individual participant. This is not to downgrade other sports, but merely to point out that although the participant can purchase his rifle, sights and bullet mould, all the rest of it – casting bullets, loading the ammunition and the actual shooting – must be done by the individual competitor. Even with the best of equipment, if the shooter and/or spotter does not comprehend the effects of the wind, mirage, changing light, humidity or even the lay of the land, he or she probably will not be in the winner's circle.

But that is what makes this game and these people so great. Rather than trying to beat or out-do another particular individual, virtually every shooter on the line is trying to better himself or herself – trying to do better than they have ever done before, trying to set a personal record. If winning the match happens to be the result of a personal record, so much the better. But I can promise you, any and every shooter who ever fired a higher score than they had ever fired before, regardless of what that score is, feels a surge of exhilaration that says "By golly, I've done it!"

Then there is one other deep rooted driving impulse

that makes shooting the black powder cartridge rifle so intoxicating or addictive. It is the feeling of standing in the footsteps of those who went before us over 100 years ago, the knowledge that you are holding a rifle just like the rifle Billy Dixon, "Moccasin" Jim Stell, John Cook and a host of others used back in the 1870s to open up the West. It is knowing that like they often did, you have cast your own bullets and loaded your own black-powder cartridges and now, like them, you have to put yourself and your skills to the test. When you hear that Sharps or rolling block hammer to full cock, you hear exactly the same metallic "click" those old-timers heard so many years ago. You smell the same powder smoke, and you feel the same sense of self-accomplishment when your target falls from its stand 547 yards distant. And over that dark abyss of time, you can almost hear voices of the past whispering in your mind of a job well done, a faint touch on your shoulder that says, "We are glad you remember!"

Dr. Peter L. Fry of Australia (left) and Ron Snover at the BPCR silhouette National Championship Match at Raton, New Mexico, August 2000. These are two of the finest gentlemen you will ever meet.

"The tortures of that icy seat could make a Spartan sob,"
– from *The Passing of The Backhouse*, author unknown.

New facilities at the Wilton, New York, Rod and Gun Club range, circa 2000.

Other books by Paul A. Matthews:

Forty Years with the .45-70

The Paper Jacket

Loading the Black Powder Rifle Cartridge

Shooting the Black Powder Cartridge Rifle

How-To's for the Black Powder Cartridge Rifle Shooter

Cast Bullets for the Black Powder Cartridge Rifle

Wind Drift and Deceleration of the Cast Bullet at Black-Powder Velocities

Casting Premium Bullets for the Black Powder Cartridge Rifle

Wolfe Publishing's editing and production staff:

Publisher: Mark Harris

Editorial: Roberta Montgomery
Dixie Wenger

Cover Design: Gerald Hudson

Production Design: Becky Pinkley